BLOSSOM

BLOSSOM

30-DAY DEVOTIONAL

Brandy Baucom

ISBN: 9781695875692

DEDICATION

This devotional was written in dedication to my daughter, Callie and my niece, Ella. God has big plans for both of you. My prayer is that you will allow Him to use the passion, strength, and independence that He blessed you with to proudly shine your lights for the world to see!

Love, Mom/Aunt Brandy

TABLE OF CONTENTS

INTRODUCTION

Too often, girls set self-expectations based on what the world thinks is important; looks, wealth, popularity, and stuff. The world tells us that the only way to be beautiful is by fitting in a size 2, wearing the expensive clothes, while driving the coolest car, and talking on the coolest I-phone. The world says that to be popular, we must do what the popular kids do, which most of the time are not in line with the word of God. When this happens, girls that once dreamed of their future begin to worry about whether they are good enough. We start trying to change ourselves to fit the mold of what other people think we should be. The pressure that we put ourselves under can lead to stress, anxiety, and depression. We try too hard to fit in, when we were born to stand out.

We are called to STAND OUT, not to blend into the darkness of the world. With Jesus as our Savior, we are DIFFERENT. He sets us apart in a world that pressures us to conform. He sees our beauty based on our souls and not on physical appearance.

We need to base our self-worth not on the world's opinion, but on what our Savior says are important qualities. We should care more about the opinion of the One that created us than what the "popular" crowd says is in.

Do you feel like you don't fit in? Do you feel pressured to look and dress a certain way? Do you wonder why you are the only one in a circle of friends that hasn't given in to the temptation to make the wrong choices? Or have you been spending too much time focusing on the outside view of yourself and of others? Do you need a reminder of who God is and who you are called to be?

BLOSSOM

In this 30-day devotional, we are going to delve into God's Word to find out exactly who God says that we are and learn how to combat the constant pressures that are so prevalent in the lives of young girls and women today. Hopefully, at the end of our journey, we will look back and realize that we are worth far more than rubies and gold to our Heavenly Father. I pray that even though it is difficult, we will no longer compare ourselves to the world and that we will be confident in who we are at our core, Daughters of the One True King.

Join me on this quest to find out God's purpose for us, and how to BLOSSOM into the woman that He has planned for us to be.

"BLESSED IS SHE WHO HAS BELIEVED THAT THE LORD WOULD FULFILL HIS PROMISES TO HER!"
~ LUKE 1:45 ~

WEEK 1 - WHO HE IS

Before we find out what God says about us, we need to know who He is and what He does for us.

- LOVING
- SOVEREIGN
- OMNISCIENT
- GOOD
- OMNIPRESENT

DAY 1 - LOVING

MAIN POINT

In hard times, it can be easy to look up to heaven and ask why. "God why did you let this happen? How can you say you love me and yet you keep taking things away? Are you punishing me? I don't understand why I keep failing. Why won't you take away my pain? Are you there? "But this week as we learn about the King of Kings and the Lord of Lords, we will see that He loves us even through all our doubts and fears.

SCRIPTURE

How do we know that God is loving? Let's go to the Word of Truth for the answer.

Read John 3:16.

Bottom line, when Adam and Eve ate of that apple in the Garden of Eden, man became sinners. We are born with a sinful nature and since God wants us to love Him by our own choice and not because it is a "rule", He gave us Free Will. He lets us choose how we feel about Him. He doesn't want us to be forced to love Him; He wants us to choose to. He knocks on the door and we must decide whether to open it and let Him in.

"Here I am! I stand at the door and knock. If anyone hears my voice and opens the door, I will come in and eat with that person, and they with me." ***Revelations 3:20 (NIV)***

But God is perfect and holy. He cannot sin, nor can He look upon sin, therefore because of our sin, He could not have a relationship with us. BUT he wanted to, so He sent His only Son, who was fully man and fully God, who was also blameless and pure, to take on the punishment for our sins.

Why would God do that? The answer is simple. Our sin keeps us separate from God, so when our earthly life is over, we cannot be with Him in Heaven. We are destined for an eternal separation from our Creator in Hell, a place where one second will feel like an eternity. There will be a lake of fire and pain and suffering will be endless.

"For the wages of sin is death, but the gift of God is eternal life in Christ Jesus our Lord." **Romans 6:23 (NIV)**

LIFE APPLICATION

God sent His Son Jesus to take on our sin and shame so that we could be clean and righteous and therefore have fellowship with Him. With that relationship and because of the sacrifice of Jesus, we can one day spend eternity in Heaven, all because Jesus took the blame for our bad choices.

God loves us so much that didn't want to be apart from us, so He made a way that we could be with Him. That way was allowing His only Son to die hanging from a cross that He didn't deserve to be on. Jesus went through his earthly life proclaiming that God is love and man spat on Him. Jesus preached forgiveness and the people mocked Him. Jesus preached about the Kingdom of Heaven and man killed Him. God knew that all of this would happen. He wasn't taken by surprise. This was why He had sent Jesus in the first place. He didn't want us to have to go to Hell, so He gave up Jesus for us.

What an amazing love!!! This is not a love that will ever change based on mood or time; this is an eternal love. One that cannot be taken away or lessened. All that He wants in return is for us to love Him back. So, he gives us the option to accept Him or not. Do we believe and accept what He sent Jesus to do or will we spit on Him and His offering like the people who crucified Jesus?

Will we submit our own lives to Him to do with as He pleases? If so, we must accept Jesus as our Savior and ask Him to save us from Hell?

"If you declare with your mouth, "Jesus is Lord," and believe in your heart that God raised him from the dead, you will be saved. For it is with your heart that you believe and are justified, and it is with your mouth that you profess your faith and are saved." ***Romans 10:9-10 (NIV)***

And once we do that, Jesus stands in between us and God. He is our advocate, claiming us as His and therefore holding our place in Heaven until we get there.

"Yet to all who did receive him, to those who believed in his name, he gave the right to become children of God – children born not of natural descent, nor of human decision or a husband's will, but born of God." ***John 1:12-13 (NIV)***

What kind of love are you looking for? Are you looking for someone that puts your needs before their own and makes sacrifices for you? What about someone that is willing to give their life for you? A love that wants what is best for you? Well, Jesus is the man for you. I pray that if you have not already, that you will ask Jesus to come into your life and save you. It is the best decision that you will ever make.

There are hundreds of verses, songs, prayers, and psalms that speak of His undying, unchanging love for us. What a great Lord that we serve!

Let's look at a few of them.

Psalm 136:26 His love endures forever!

There will never be a point in your life, no matter how far you stray from Him, that He will ever stop loving you.

Romans 8:35-39 His love is always there!

Neither life nor death, trouble nor famine can separate us from His love.

Psalm 119:76 His love is comforting!

His love provides peace and hope in the good times and the bad.

Psalm 13:5 His love is unfailing and trustworthy!

We can trust that He always knows what is best.

He longs for us to be the Spirit led, faithful women that He knew ahead of time that we would be. He has work chosen specifically for you to do that will further His Kingdom and lead others into a closer fellowship with Him. You have a purpose. He didn't take away any of your free will, but He already knew what your choices would be.

CHALLENGE

The future that God has in store for us is far better than anything we could imagine for ourselves. He intends for us to grow into Godly, bold women that call on Him as our unshakable Rock in times of struggle.

He wants us to tell other people about His great love and shout the Gospel for all to hear. He has a future planned where we live according to His truths, rather than false truths the world wants us to believe. He desires to be our guide to show the lost that hope with Jesus is eternal and cannot be extinguished by any circumstance. Will there be trials and struggles? Of course! But we can make it through hard times by focusing on the promises He gives in His

Word. The promises of His unchanging, never ending love, no matter how much we fail or question. Sometimes bad things happen. The bible says very clearly that we WILL have problems. It never says that the journey will be easy. But what it does say over and over, is how much He loves us and that we will never regret a life lived in Christ.

PRAYER

Heavenly Father, we thank you for your awesome love for us. Thank you that you always remain the same, no matter how much we change. There is nothing that can ever separate us from You, and we pray that we can have open and receptive hearts as we search your Word for the truths. Be with us, Lord, as we seek a deeper relationship with you and guide us on how to bloom into the women that you intend for us to be. In Jesus Name, Amen.

"THOUGH THE MOUNTAINS BE SHAKEN, AND THE HILLS BE REMOVED, YET MY UNFAILING LOVE FOR YOU WILL NOT BE SHAKEN...SAYS THE LORD, WHO HAS COMPASSION ON YOU."

~ ISAIAH 54:10 ~

DAY 2 - SOVEREIGN

MAIN POINT

We will not fully comprehend the power of God until we become one with Him in Heaven one day. The possibilities of His endless power are far beyond what our earthly minds can fathom. We can only think through human eyes and therefore have no concept of the abilities or depth of God. He oversees everything. While He had the power and might to create the universe, He can also end it, and one day He will. There is no one like our God. He knows every single thought, word, and breath that has happened from the beginning of time until now. He makes the sun rise every morning and set in the evening. He has protected His people throughout time in mighty ways, even when we turned our backs on Him. There is no greater power or boundless love than His. Even the rocks cry out in praise for Him, so shouldn't we?

SCRIPTURE

Let's find out from the Bible about His great power and authority.

And said, "Lord, the God of our ancestors, are you not the God who is in heaven? You rule over all the kingdoms of the nations. Power and might are in Your hand, and no one can withstand you."
2 Chronicles 20:6 (NIV)

"The earth is the LORD's, and everything in it, the world, and all who live in it; for he founded it on the seas and established it on the waters." ***Psalm 24:1-2 (NIV)***

"He is before all things, and in him all things hold together" ***Colossians 1:17 (NIV)***

SCRIPTURE

In learning more about who God is, let's go deeper into His Word to gain specific insight. What better way to see what He is capable of in the future than to see what things He has done in the past.

Book of Esther - God chose Esther to be the new queen for King Xerxes. God knew that she was faithful and would be the queen who eventually saved the Jewish people from a plan to destroy them. He had also provided for her to be raised by an uncle who would be Esther's helper in saving God's chosen people.

Exodus - With Moses, God spoke through a burning bush, parted the Red Sea, made food fall from the sky, water come from a rock, and His presence guided all the Israelites by a cloud in the sky.

Genesis - What about Joseph? God allowed Joseph to be bullied by his brothers and thrown into a well, sent to prison, falsely accused of rape, and then eventually was raised back up to be one of the most powerful men in Egypt. God had a mighty plan for Joseph.

Daniel - He closed the mouths of lions so that they wouldn't harm Daniel after he was thrown into the den for praying to God. He protected Shadrach, Meshach, and Abednego from the fiery furnace after they refused to worship an idol. They came out of the furnace not even smelling like smoke.

1 Samuel - He helped a young David defeat a giant Philistine who was opposing the Israelites with just 5 little stones.

LIFE APPLICATION

There are so many more completely awesome illustrations of God's infinite power and might in scripture to remind us that when we don't know what to do, we can trust Him. He has shown time and time again that He protects His people. He demonstrates His great love by sending Jesus to save us, so there is no doubt that He always has our best interest in mind.

Many times, in life, circumstances happen that can leave us feeling un-anchored and helpless. Here are a few examples of trying circumstances that we can go through:

- Sickness or injury
- Parents getting divorced
- Failing classes
- A bad break-up
- Someone close to us dying
- Parent losing a job
- Failure
- Depression/Anxiety

Think of something in your own life that left you feeling helpless and weak?

Let me assure you that not only does God care about every single tear that you have cried over this, but He has every intention of using that circumstance to mature you in your spiritual walk. When bad or worrisome things happen, we can rest assured in the fact that He is in control over everything. That may not mean that He always takes away the problem though. Sometimes he allows us to go through difficult circumstances to show us how much we need Him and to strengthen our trust in Him.

When these things occur, it is very easy to run and hide, burying our head in the sand until it gets better. But God wants us to take these situations and hand them over to Him. He tells us to stop worrying about them and let Him handle it all. He wants us to remember that in all things, He loves us, He is faithful, and that He will never leave our side. While these realizations don't make the problems come less often or hurt any less, letting go of the worry and having faith that He is in His control can help us make it through the hardest of days.

God promises that He is out for your good. He wants you to trust in Him for all your needs, whether spiritual or physical. Today we have seen that by His awesome and mighty power, His plans will be accomplished. So why spend our lives running away or fighting against what He knows is best for us?

"I KNOW THAT YOU CAN DO ALL THINGS; NO PURPOSE OF YOURS CAN BE THWARTED." ***JOB 42:2 (NIV)***

What does sovereign mean to you?

According to www.dictionary.com, "*sovereignty is the quality or state of having supreme power or authority.*"

This means that God doesn't answer to anyone. He always has the final word, the final decision. He has supreme control over everything. He could make us do anything that He pleases, and rather than forcing us to love and worship Him, He gives us the ability to choose. He wants us to love Him by our own free will.

PRAYER

Dear Lord, we cannot even fathom the entirety of your power. We know that nothing is impossible with You. Thank you for being in control of our circumstances and fears. We know that we can trust You with everything. Please give us peace through difficult times so that we may learn to lean on You for everything that we need. In Jesus's name, Amen.

DAY 3 - OMNISCIENT

MAIN POINT

Omniscient means all-knowing. God knows everything, there is nothing that you can hide from him. Whether it's your darkest secret or most sinful thought, He knows it all. From the beginning of time until now, there is nothing that is out of his reach. He knows your needs, desires, fears, insecurities, and He has a plan to use them for His glory, and so that you can become the woman that He wants you to be.

LIFE APPLICATION

Think for a second about your biggest secret, you know the one that you would never tell even your closest friends. The most secretive thing that you wouldn't want anyone to ever know about you. Now imagine that someone found out.

How would you feel? What are you afraid that they would think? Now I want you to realize that God already knows. He already knows every single one of your secrets, and fears. He already knows exactly what you don't want the world to know, and why. And above all else, not only does He still love you, but if you have received Jesus as your Savior, there is not one single thing that you could ever do that isn't covered by the mercy and grace that God gives. Your sins are wiped clean. Jesus already paid your price!

IF GOD KNOWS ALL OF OUR NEEDS, THEN WHY DO WE NEED TO PRAY?

God uses prayer, as a way for us to communicate with him. We don't have very many close friends with whom we don't talk to. What kind of friendship would that be?

Billy Graham said it this way, *"Prayer is simply a two-way conversation between you and God."*

SCRIPTURE

"Nothing in all creation is hidden from God's sight. Everything is uncovered and laid bare before the eyes of him to whom we must give account" ***Hebrews 4:13 (NIV)***

Psalm 139:4 "Before a word is on my tongue, you, Lord know it completely."

Psalm 139:1-3 "You have searched me; Lord and you know me. You know when I sit and when I rise; you perceive my thoughts from afar. You discern my going out and my lying down; you are familiar with all my ways."

Luke 12:7 "Indeed, the very hairs of your head are all numbered. Don't be afraid; you are worth more than many sparrows."

I want you to notice in that last verse, Luke 12:7, that not only does He know everything about you, but you are WORTH much to Him. You are important to the Creator of the Universe. In 1 Samuel 16:7 we see that God doesn't look at outward appearance.

"But the Lord said to Samuel, "Do not consider his appearance or his height, for I have rejected him. The Lord does not look at the things people look at. People look at the outward appearance, but the LORD looks at the heart." ***1 Samuel 16:7 (NIV)***

He isn't restricted to seeing what you present to the world to see. You cannot fool the Lord. Physical beauty, material wealth, popularity, God doesn't care whether you have the most friends in the class or drive the coolest car. He cares about the state of your soul. He cares about who you are deep down when no one is around. Have you accepted Him? If so, are you walking with Him and maturing with every passing day? Are you trying to treat people with kindness and love as Jesus did? Are you sharing the good news of the Gospel with those around you by living a life of servitude rather than self-importance? He cares about who you are at your very core, not what you show to the world.

CHALLENGE

Today think about this question. Are you showing everyone the true you? The you that Jesus knows. Do you walk and talk the same way with your parents that you do with friends? Do you say things behind people's backs that you would never want them to find out about? Are you the same person in public that you are behind closed doors, when it is just you and Jesus? I want you to consider your relationship with Him and how you can remain true to your faith while out in the world and distracted by the devil's evil schemes to trip you up. Think of some ways that you can show more of your truth and light in the world?

PRAYER

Lord, we only show the world what we want them to see, but You see through all of it. We are so grateful that You love us so much. You know all our secrets and don't run away. You know all our fears and don't laugh. You know all our sins and love us anyway. Thank You for who You are and how we can show You our hearts without fear. Please help us to have the courage to tell others about Your never-ending love and the hope that we have in You. In Jesus Name we pray. Amen.

DAY 4 - GOOD

MAIN POINT

In our journey to know our Lord better, today we arrive at His goodness. The Bible tells us that every good thing good comes from above. We must remember daily that the world's version of good and God's version are two totally different concepts. God's version of good is truth and purity, while the world's is based on feelings. Feelings change, but God remains the same. He simply is. The world's version of good changes based on what is popular or what feels good at the time. Fifty years ago, homosexuality was considered wrong in the eyes of the world, but today the world says that it should be applauded. The world is constantly changing, altering its views based on what people want and find important right now. God's goodness is an eternal, unchanging, steadfast truth. As children of God, we need to remain in His Word to know how to be pure and holy in God's eyes rather than what other people think and say. Throughout Scripture, we can find hundreds of verses that speak about God's goodness and light.

SCRIPTURE

"Give thanks to the Lord, for He is good; his love endures forever." **1 Chronicles 16:34 (NIV)**

"You, Lord, are forgiving and good, abounding in love to all who call to you." **Psalm 86:5 (NIV)**

"The Lord is good to all, he has compassion on all he has made." ***Psalm 145:9 (NIV)***

Not only can we see His goodness, but also that He wants good things for us, his children.

Romans 8:28 "And we know that in all things God works for the good of those who love him, who have been called according to his purpose."

2 Peter 1:3 "His divine power has given us everything we need for a godly life through our knowledge of him, who called us by his own glory and goodness."

Jeremiah 29:11 "For I know the plans I have for you," declares the Lord, "plans to prosper you and not to harm you, plans to give you hope and a future."

LIFE APPLICATION

He has big plans for us! Does this mean that everything is always going to go our way and that there will never be any disappointment? Definitely not, but what it does mean is that His gifts and blessings are given based on His perfect Will and He will disperse them as He sees fit. He gives them based on how they will most benefit your walk with Him or His walk with someone else.

It is tempting sometimes to see things from our worldly perspective and to forget that He knows best. We are constantly bombarded on TV and Social Media with pictures of what we "should" be like.

Let's say, for instance that you want to go to a specific college. You have worked hard to get in, your grades are great, your essay is spot-on, your interview went well, you think you are a shoo-in, but then you get the rejection letter in the mail. It can be very frustrating to want something so badly, and it not work out the way we think it should.

But God sees things differently than we do. He sees things from an eternal view while we see them as we are most familiar, temporal. He might see that at a different college, your relationship with Him will flourish into what He always intended. Or that He could show you a future career path from the college that He sets for you, or He knows that you will meet your future spouse. He is the God of the entire universe after all, He can see a 360-degree map of your life and where He wants it to lead. Our place as His children is to accept that He is working things out for our good even though we cannot see the ending. Even when we cannot see it, He can, and He is trustworthy.

Let's take a moment and ask the Lord to give us a greater trust in His goodness, no matter the circumstance.

PRAYER

Lord, we just thank you for your infinite goodness. You are such an awesome God, the way that you provide everything that we need and protect us even when we don't realize it. Thank you for sending your Son, Jesus to die for our sins. We pray that as we attempt to walk through this life in Your way, that we will seek you and your truths first and that when things don't work out the way that we think they should, we will trust you to know what is best for us. It's hard for us when we can't see why things happen the way that they do but help us to put our faith completely in You, so that we can live Your way instead of ours. In Jesus' name, Amen.

DAY 5 - OMNIPRESENT

MAIN POINT

"Omnipresent - to be present in all places at all times."
Miriam Webster

Another trait of God is that He can be anywhere at any time. But when we really take the time to consider the enormity of that statement, our minds simply cannot comprehend it. The fact that God can be here with me, knowing my every thought while simultaneously being there with all His other children in the world at the same time. It is a staggering realization.

As humans, we know that if we are in the classroom at school, then we cannot be at home in the living room as well. It's either or, not both. But for God, this rule doesn't exist. He is not bound by the restraints that we are. He can be anywhere and everywhere all at the same time, every second of every day. He doesn't need time to sleep. He is God. He can comfort me in my sadness at the very same moment that He is giving courage to someone else who needs it. His power and might are beyond anything that we can imagine.

Let's think about the fact that there are no off-limits places or abilities for God. Whether you are in a group of 500 people or alone in the hidden spaces of your mind, there is no desert big enough and no river wide enough that He cannot reach you. You cannot be "bad" enough for Him to give up on you, but you also cannot be "good" enough to earn His love. His love and presence just are. They are always present no matter what type of day you are having, no matter how angry or hurt that you may be, even if it's toward God Himself. There is no hidden space that you could withdraw to that He cannot find you and bring you back to Him. If He can be everywhere simultaneously then that means that we will never be alone. So, we never have to fear being without Him, because He is always there.

SCRIPTURE

Let's look at a few of the verses that show the omnipresence of God.

Jeremiah 23:24 "Who can hide in secret places so that I cannot see them?" declares the Lord. "Do not I fill heaven and earth?" declares the Lord."

Psalm 139:7 "Where can I go from your Spirit? Where can I flee from your presence?"

Job 34:21 "His eyes are on the ways of mortals; he sees their every step"

Proverbs 15:3 "The eyes of the Lord are everywhere, keeping watch on the wicked and the good."

Let's think about the Holy Trinity for a second. There are three parts of God; the Father, the Son, and the Holy Spirit. Once we accept Jesus into our hearts then the Holy Spirit comes to live within us. Therefore, not only is God always watching, and Jesus always at our defense, but the Holy Spirit is literally living inside of us and thus, He is with us no matter where we go. We are never alone.

LIFE APPLICATION

What does this information mean for me?

The fact that God is everywhere means that ...

On my worst day, when I cannot get the words out because my heart is so discouraged and hurt, He knows my heart. He was there and saw what happened. He knows the ins and outs of the situation even better than I do. He knows why it occurred and how it will be resolved. So, when we cry out to Him in prayer, but can't find the words to explain, let's remember that He already knows, and He has a plan to work it out for my good.

"And we know that in all things God works for the good of those who love him, who have been called according to his purpose." ***Romans 8:28 (NIV)***

When I stumble and doubt Him or even turn away from His love, He is still there. He still knows what is in my heart. And He will stay with me, reminding me who He is, how much He loves me, and that I belong to Him. He will draw me back to Himself where I belong, no matter how long it takes. I am one of His children.

"What do you think? If a man owns a hundred sheep, and one of them wanders away, will he not leave the ninety-nine on the hills and go to look for the one that wandered off?" ***Matthew 18:12 (NIV)***

It is amazing to think that we who are merely a "vapor in the wind" matter to the Lord of the Earth. That He cares enough about each of us that He wants us to know that we are never without His presence and love, no matter what.

"WHEN YOU PASS THROUGH THE WATERS, I WILL BE WITH YOU..." ***ISAIAH 43:2 (NIV)***

CHALLENGE

Today as you go about your normal day-to-day responsibilities, take a moment throughout your day to consider the Lord being present with you. He is there as you get up and get your day started, He is there during all your arguments. He is there when you are alone. He is there when you are tempted to try that first drug, and He is there when you resist. He is with you through it all, and He is watching you with very closely with pride, and a love that only your Heavenly Father can have.

PRAYER:

Most Gracious Heavenly Father, we are humbled that you love us this much. We mess up so often, yet you never leave us alone to wander this world without You. In this life we will inevitably face darkness, please help us to look to You alone for the light to guide our path. In Jesus' Name, Amen.

"SO DO NOT FEAR, FOR I AM WITH YOU..."
~ ISAIAH 41:10 ~

WEEK 2 - WHO HE SAYS WE ARE

Now that we have a clear understanding of some of the qualities of God, let's find out how He views us.

- UNIQUE
- BEAUTIFUL
- VALUABLE
- POWERFUL
- PROTECTED

DAY 6 - UNIQUE

I AM HIS. This week I want you to understand something. Your identity is NOT who others say you are. Your identity is who God says that you are. No matter what those girls at school said, no matter whether that boy likes you, if you were laughed at today, and even if you were the bully, you are loved by the King of Kings and the Lord of Lords. He sent His Son to die for you, so that you didn't have to go to Hell for eternity.

Think about that for a second. No matter what anyone else in the world thinks or says, you are adored by your Creator. One promise that you can fully count on is that your Heavenly Father is truth. He is holy and therefore no deceit can be within Him. To Him, you are His beloved girl! And the only opinion of you that will remain is the one that lasts for eternity.

"So that he who blesses himself in the earth shall bless himself in the God of truth; And he who swears in the earth shall swear by the God of truth; Because the former troubles are forgotten, and because they are hidden from My eyes!" ***Isaiah 65:16 (NKJV)***

MAIN POINT

When God created and breathed life into us, we were all uniquely made in His image. The Bible says in Psalm 147:4 that He chose the number of stars and calls them each by name. How amazing! He chose to give you life. He thought that the darkness of the world needed your light. If He knows every single one of the billions of stars in the sky by name, you can rest assured that He also knows every detail about you, and you are far more important to Him than a star.

"HE DETERMINES THE NUMBER OF THE STARS AND CALLS THEM EACH BY NAME." **PSALM 147:4 (NIV)**

There is no other that was made like you. You are one of a kind. He knew you before you were born and created you with a specific personality. He chose your parents, your future friends, your nationality, your gender, race, and after He created you, He saw that it was good! (Genesis 1:31)

He knew what your strengths would be and what areas that you would need His help the most. He knew when you would accept Jesus as your Savior, what your individual testimony would be, and how you would use it for His glory. He knew the exact times in life that you would specifically need His comfort, His correction, His wisdom, and His strength. But on the flip side, He also knew when He would need to pick you up and carry you through the most difficult of circumstances. He knows the very number of hairs on your head and he knit you together in the exact way that he wanted you to be.

You were CHOSEN by God to be a part of His plan.

"I PRAISE YOU BECAUSE I AM FEARFULLY AND WONDERFULLY MADE; YOUR WORKS ARE WONDERFUL, I KNOW THAT FULL WELL. **PSALM 139:14 (NIV)**

Inside of you there is something that is yours and yours alone. Are you a good listener or a good encourager? Are you a peacemaker? Do you see through the outer "shell" that others put on as a front to protect themselves from being vulnerable? Are you good with children or musically talented? No matter what your gifts are, God has a plan to use YOU to reach someone else. When God is at work in someone, He makes miracles happen!

Take a moment and think about your own life. What talents and gifts did the Lord bless you with?

Now think about ways that He can use them to spread the Gospel.

Everyone has a talent. How do I know? Because the Lord has a purpose for each one of us. You might not have realized what it is yet, but in His time, He will reveal it to you.

"THERE IS A TIME FOR EVERYTHING, AND A SEASON FOR EVERY ACTIVITY UNDER THE HEAVENS..." **ECCLESIASTES 3:1 (NIV)**

As a teenager, I was not yet a child of God and so I didn't have the benefit of knowing that He'd made me special and unique. Later, when He saved me, the Holy Spirit began to mold me into the woman that unbeknownst to me, God had been planning all along. He began to use several traits in me, that I now know are spiritual gifts and talents to reach others. Before I met Jesus, I didn't even know to look.

SCRIPTURE

Check out some of these examples of how the skills and abilities that God gives His people were used for His glory in the Bible.

Genesis:41	Joseph could decipher dreams.
2 Samuel 22	David wrote psalms and played the harp.
Exodus 3:12	Moses had the very presence of the Lord helping him to bring the Israelites out of Egypt.
Exodus 4:16	Aaron was a great speaker.
1 Kings 3:12	King Solomon had wisdom.
Judges 14:5-6	Samson had super strength.

LIFE APPLICATION

These are just some examples of the abilities that God provided His people. These were in the Old Testament, but there are many more all through His Word. God asked all these people to use their gifts for His plan and purpose. There will be many times in your Christian walk that He will ask the same of you. You might not be asked to part the Red Sea like Moses, but He can still work miracles in the life that you lead.

Are you good with children? Would you be a good teacher? Do you participate in recreational activities where you can meet new people and show them kindness? Do you have a desire to be a doctor one day and help people through the gift of healing? Whatever your talents, God says that you are a masterpiece, created in Him for a purpose.

"FOR WE ARE GOD'S HANDIWORK, CREATED IN CHRIST JESUS TO DO GOOD WORKS, WHICH GOD PREPARED IN ADVANCE FOR US TO DO." ***EPHESIANS 2:10 (NIV)***

CHALLENGE

Take a moment today to consider the fact that you were uniquely created. No one on Earth is the exact same as you and God created you this way for a reason. You don't have to worry about what others think or say. They are not your Heavenly Father, and they don't know you like He does. He says that you are special and that you belong to Him.

PRAYER

Gracious Heavenly Father, thank you for creating us in Your image. Thank you that you made us with a specific purpose in mind. We are so humbled that you care about us enough to have a plan for our lives.

We don't have a complete picture of what will happen in the future, but with You guiding our steps, we know that we will be right in Your sight. Please give us the courage to stand firm in your truths, even when others don't. We love you Lord, Amen.

"God has formed many diamonds, but He made only one of you."
~ Darlene Sala ~

DAY 7 - BEAUTIFUL

MAIN POINT

You are His. You were created in His image. You are beautiful, smart, and amazing whether anyone else tells you that or not. In God's eyes, you are precious.

The Lord doesn't see what the world sees. He doesn't see what you consider your physical flaws. He looks far beyond that to see to the innermost being of who you are at your core. You were made in His image.

Read the following verses about your beauty.

- You are altogether beautiful, my darling; there is no flaw in you. **Song of Songs 4:7 (NIV)**

- She is clothed with strength and dignity; she can laugh at the days to come. **Proverbs 31:25 (NIV)**

- You will be a crown of splendor in the LORD's hand, a royal diadem in the hand of your God. **Isaiah 62:3 (NIV)**

- My beloved spoke and said to me, "Arise, my darling, my beautiful one, come with me. **Song of Songs 2:10 (NIV)**

- "Your beauty should not come from outward adornment, such as elaborate hairstyles and the wearing of gold jewelry or fine clothes. Rather it should be that of your inner self, the unfading beauty of a gentle and quiet spirit, which is of great worth in God's sight." **1 Peter 3:3-4 (NIV)**

Wow. What poetry in those words! This is how the Lord looks at you. He doesn't look at your hair or your eyes or your clothes, He sees your soul, and it is beautiful to Him.

SCRIPTURE

Let's learn about the Woman at the Well. **Read John 4:7-26.**

"When a Samaritan woman came to draw water, Jesus said to her, "Will you give me a drink?" (His disciples had gone into the town to buy food.) The Samaritan woman said to him, "You are a Jew and I am a Samaritan woman. How can you ask me for a drink?" (For Jews do not associate with Samaritans.

Jesus answered her, "If you knew the gift of God and who it is that asks you for a drink, you would have asked him, and he would have given you living water." "Sir," the woman said, "you have nothing to draw with and the well is deep. Where can you get this living water? Are you greater than our father Jacob, who gave us the well and drank from it himself, as did also his sons and his livestock?" Jesus answered, "Everyone who drinks this water will be thirsty again, but whoever drinks the water I give them will never thirst. Indeed, the water I give them will become in them a spring of water welling up to eternal life."

The woman said to him, "Sir, give me this water so that I won't get thirsty and have to keep coming here to draw water." He told her, "Go, call your husband and come back." "I have no husband," she replied. Jesus said to her, "You are right when you say you have no husband. The fact is, you have had five husbands, and the man you now have is not your husband. What you have just said is quite true."

"Sir," the woman said, "I can see that you are a prophet. Our ancestors worshiped on this mountain, but you Jews claim that the place where we must worship is in Jerusalem."

"Woman," Jesus replied, "believe me, a time is coming when you will worship the Father neither on this mountain nor in Jerusalem. You Samaritans worship what you do not know; we worship what we do know, for salvation is from the Jews. Yet a time is coming and has now come when the true worshipers will worship the Father in the Spirit and in truth, for they are the kind of worshipers the Father seeks. God is spirit, and his worshipers must worship in the Spirit and in truth."

The woman said, "I know that Messiah is coming. When he comes, he will explain everything to us." Then Jesus declared, "I, the one speaking to you—I am he."

LIFE APPLICATION

This story teaches a powerful lesson that every girl needs to hear. This woman was part of the Samaritan race who were despised by the Jewish people. It was not a common custom for the two to mingle, let alone have an in-depth conversation about salvation. But here was Jesus, asking her for water and telling her about eternal life.

We notice that she drank alone and from a community well, which typically meant that she was considered a social outcast in the community. She'd previously had 5 husbands and now lived with a 6th outside of wedlock. She was not considered to have high standing and was looked upon as immoral.

Yet Jesus took time to show her that it didn't matter who she'd been in the past. It didn't matter the mistakes that she'd made or how many times she'd made them. He simply offered acceptance where she stood and unconditional love. Yes, he pointed out the truth of her sin, but with a love and affection that she had probably never known. In Jesus's eyes this woman was a beautiful creation. It was only through this conversation with her that she realized the true meaning of the Living Water being offered to her.

Remember today that no matter your hair color, height, weight, gender, or race, it does not matter if the world thinks you are beautiful, because you serve a Heavenly Father that sees your beauty clearly. He loves you JUST AS YOU ARE! In His opinion, you are beautiful and valuable enough that He sent His Son to die for you.

PRAYER

Lord, we come to you today to thank You that you love us. No matter where we are in our lives, you love us just the way we are.

You stand at the door and knock and ask to come in and fellowship with us. You are so amazing! Help us to remember throughout the days of living in a world that places value on outward appearance, that you place it on our hearts. You think we are valuable and beautiful even though we are still sinners.

We love you Lord and we pray that you will help us to show others your grace and love regardless of their outside appearance. Everyone needs to know You regardless of their circumstance. In Jesus' name, Amen.

DAY 8 - VALUABLE

MAIN POINT

If you have accepted Jesus as your Savior, then the Holy Spirit has come to live inside of you. When the Holy Spirit is at work within you, you will not remain the same as you were before. It's simply not possible. The Spirit is part of the Holy Trinity, which is fully God, and therefore good, holy, and perfect. When your soul is filled with God, it begins to overflow and change you. He changes how you think, your priorities, and how you act. He slowly and lovingly molds you to be more like Jesus, and over time we start to exhibit more and more of the qualities of those qualities. God changes people. Not out of fear or by anything that we ourselves do, but because you cannot be filled with all that love without some of it bubbling over and overflowing from you.

"Above all else, guard your heart, for everything you do flows from it." **Proverbs 4:23 (NIV)**

When you realize the depths and the width of His affection for you, you cannot help but be eternally changed. The fact that He loves us so much even though we mess up all the time should be reason enough to want to please Him. To God, you are more precious than even the rarest diamonds. You are important to Him and He will never stop loving you. You become His completely...His beloved.

SCRIPTURE

"She is more precious than rubies; nothing you desire can compare with her. Long life is in her right hand; in her left hand are riches and honor. Her ways are pleasant ways and all her paths are peace. She is a tree of life to those who take hold of her; those who hold her fast will be blessed." ***Proverbs 3:15-18 (NIV)***

LIFE APPLICATION

This is how your Savior speaks about YOU! He says you are precious and rare! Friend, I want you to hear today that you are VALUABLE to God. The world is constantly beating us down to the point that sometimes it's difficult to see through all the lies, and you may not feel valuable, but it's in His Word in black and white. You are PRECIOUS to Him. He wants you to live in Him and trust His ways because you are important and worth more than the most priceless gems. Take a moment and think about this truth!

"SINCE YOU ARE PRECIOUS AND HONORED IN MY SIGHT, AND BECAUSE I LOVE YOU…" **Isaiah 43:4 (NIV)**

Let's face it, without His love, we would still be destined for Hell. I am so thankful that He considers us His.

Martin Luther said it this way "God doesn't love us because of our worth, we are of worth because God loves us!"

God doesn't expect you to be perfect. He expects you to trust Him to forgive you when you mess up, so that He can make you clean again!

CHALLENGE

Forgive yourself for the past. Move forward with the intention of living a life worthy to be called a child of God. Remember to fill your heart with the things of God and He will overflow from you and then others will see Him in you.

PRAYER

Thank you, Father for loving us enough to save us. We know that we don't deserve any of the grace that you give us, and we are humbled by the fact that after everything, we are still important to you. Helps us to live lives that are pleasing to you. Give us a heart to share your love with others. Amen.

"I CAN NEVER CEASE TO WONDER THAT GOD HAS ELECTED ME."
~ C.H. SPURGEON ~

DAY 9 - POWERFUL

MAIN POINT

You are powerful, not because of anything that you could do, but simply because Jesus lives in you. The Holy Spirit is changing you, molding you, and making you more like Christ. He will give you the ability to do many things that you never could imagine. Simply put, I am not a writer, or even a creative person, but God took a willing heart and used me as a vessel to bring Him glory in this devotional that I never could have written apart from Him.

God uses broken and flawed people to do his work. He takes the unqualified and makes them qualified. Why does He do this, do you think? It seems much simpler to take someone who already has a knack, and perfect that talent for His purpose rather than starting from the ground up.

But God doesn't do easy. God does the impossible! He does things that are in-explainable, because then we have no other choice but to see His power and might through it. We cannot explain it away as being possible by human hands. For example, when someone is deathly ill with cancer and the doctors say there is no hope, but somehow the next scans reveal that the person's body is cancer-free, the doctors have no explanation. They could not have fixed this cancer ridden body themselves. The only possible rationale is that God is at work and this causes people to re-examine their beliefs. They must come to terms with the fact that God does exist if they didn't already believe.

As a young adult, I was always good with children. They were a passion that I felt God had given me. I can get a crying baby to laugh within 30 seconds, just by being my dorky self. I was also an introverted scaredy-cat when it came to being a leader in any capacity. But, as my relationship with Jesus began to mature and grow stronger, I could see that He was calling me to step out on faith and trust that His plan was stronger than my fears. Eventually, with His gentle nudging, I opened my heart up whatever He had in store. From there, He placed me in a role that I had never imagined. I became the Children's Ministry Director of my home church.

For the next three years, God called me to constantly step out of my comfort zone to speak in public, become a leader of many events, and to vocally talk about my faith by teaching children about Jesus. But this was just the beginning. He knew that if He had shown me His next plan of leading Women's Bible Studies and writing devotionals to encourage other Christians, that I would have run for the hills. I would have had a panic attack just thinking about it. As usual, He knew me better than I knew myself, and His timing was perfect.

None of this was to my own credit, this was because my Lord had chosen to give me an ability that I could use to further His kingdom and He knew that my heart was receptive and ready to His molding.

"That the God of our Lord Jesus Christ, the Father of glory, may give you a spirit of wisdom and of revelation in the knowledge of him, having the eyes of your hearts enlightened, that you may know what is the hope to which he has called you, what are the riches of his glorious inheritance in the saints..." ***Ephesians 1:17-18 (ESV)***

SCRIPTURE

Let's review some of the powerful things that God has done through His people.

- Moses parted the Red Sea so that the Israelites could get through safely to the other side.
- Elijah was taken up to heaven on a chariot of fire.

- Joshua marched around the city of Jericho for 6 days as directed. On the seventh day, the Lord made the walls of Jericho fall to the ground.
- God restored Samson and gave him the strength to crush the Philistines to death by pushing down the walls of the temple.

The fact that our God is so mighty and powerful, reminds us that He is in control of all things. We can trust Him in every situation to be full of goodness and justice, and to see His plan through to completion.

"Now to Him who is able to do immeasurably more than all we ask or imagine, according to His power that is at work within us..." **Ephesians 3:20 (NIV)**

CHALLENGE

Have you ever just sat and thought about all the blessings that you've been given? It is through His love that he provides far more than we could ever ask for. Let's go throughout our day today, giving praise and honor to the one that gives to us far more than we could ever imagine.

PRAYER

God, sometimes in the busyness of life, we forget to look up. It's so easy to go about our day without remembering that you gave it to us. Thank you for loving and providing for us. Make our hearts more willing to step as far out of our comfort zone as we need to. Teach us to remember that Your mighty power provides all the courage and ability that are needed to do Your Will. In Jesus' Name, Amen.

'JESUS SAID TO HER, "I AM THE RESURRECTION AND THE LIFE. THE ONE WHO BELIEVES IN ME WILL LIVE, EVEN THOUGH THEY DIE;"'

~ JOHN 11:25 ~

DAY 10 - PROTECTED

MAIN POINT

When you give your life to Christ and accepted Him as your Savior, you become His. You are His beloved and He is your God. Merciful and Graceful is He who saves us, but in this chapter, we are going to concentrate on how we are protected by Him. There are so many examples of God's protection of His people in the Word of God. But let's focus on the story of Rahab and how God's works for the good of those who love Him.

SCRIPTURE

Read Joshua 2:1-15.

The Israelites were camped outside the walls of Jericho, trying to find a way to invade on their way to the Promised Land. Their leader, Joshua sent two men to be spies and search out the weaknesses of the city walls. They came to the house of a prostitute named Rahab. She gave them a place to stay. The king of Jericho received word that the spies were at Rahab's house and he sent his guards to get them.

At this point. Rahab had a choice, obey the king or step out on faith in the Lord, and protect the men from certain death. She chose to hide them and send the guards in a different direction searching for them. She had heard about the Israelites, and all the miracles that God had done through Moses. She had a yearning to know Him and she realized that God was going to allow the Israelites to take over Jericho. Later, she asked the men to spare her and her family when they returned to take over Jericho, because she had saved their lives.

"But Joshua spared Rahab the prostitute, with her family and all who belonged to her, because she hid the men Joshua had sent as spies to Jericho—and she lives among the Israelites to this day." **Joshua 6:25 (NIV)**

On the day of the battle, when Israel conquered Jericho and the walls fell, everyone in the city was destroyed except for Rahab and her family. They were saved, and then made their new home with the Israelites and the One True God became Her God.

God knew of Rahab's desire to know Him. It was not by accident that the two spies came to her door. God had a plan to protect the spies as well as Rahab and her family. She was chosen and protected by the Lord, no matter her sin, and she was forever transformed by the changing that God did within her.

Here are some biblical examples of when God protected His people and what He protected them from:

- **Daniel 6:22** Daniel was protected from LIONS when God shut their mouths so that they could not bite Daniel.

- **1 Samuel 17:4** David was protected from GOLIATH. Goliath was far stronger than David, but God was on his side.

- **Genesis 37:26-27** Joseph was protected from HIS BROTHERS. Joseph was thought to be dead, but God had a plan and protected Joseph's life.

- **Exodus 2:3** Moses was protected from DEATH when the king decreed that all baby Hebrew boys be put to death.

"So do not fear, for I am with you; do not be dismayed, for I am your God. I will strengthen you and help you; I will uphold you with my righteous right hand." ***Isaiah 41:10 (NIV)***

As we end this week of WHO YOU ARE, I want you to know that even if you don't believe it of yourself, or no one else every says it to you, you can believe it because God says it is true. You are who He says you are - His child- and He WILL protect those who are His.

Prayer

Heavenly Father, we come to you today humbled by your power and love for us. We thank You that we never have to fear because you are always near. We ask that you help us to remember in times of uncertainty, that You are our strength and our protector and that You always keep your promises. Amen.

"FOR HE WILL COMMAND HIS ANGELS CONCERNING YOU TO GUARD YOU IN ALL YOUR WAYS."
~ PSALM 91:11 ~

WEEK 3 - THE WHAT

WHAT DOES GOD WANT ME TO DO? HE WANTS TO USE YOU TO GROW HIS KINGDOM!

Believe it or not, God uses the broken and the unqualified to fulfill His purpose in the world. His purpose is that as many lost people as possible have a relationship with Him. He wants them to know Him and love Him. He wants to use us to show the love to them that Jesus showed when He came to down from Heaven to die for us.

Does God need our help? No, He is the author and creator of all the world. He can move mountains and form planets. He knows all and everything good comes from Him. He can do anything that He pleases, including take away our free will, but He chooses not to.

Why? Wouldn't it be easier to just force everyone to love Him? Yes, I'm sure it would, but the reality is that our God doesn't want us to love Him because we HAVE to. He wants us to serve Him because we realize how much He loves us, and we WANT to. He wants to be our number one priority.

After all, that's how everything started. He created Adam and Eve to be perfect and sinless, and have full access to Him, but more than anything He wanted our love in return. He gave us the ability to make our own choices and decide for ourselves whether we will follow Him.

You say, "I have accepted Him already. What does this have to do with me?"

Well, here it is... The lifelong purpose of a Christian: God wants to use YOU to bring others to HIMSELF. Of course, God could come down and speak with us from a burning bush like He did with Moses, or blind us on the Damascus Road like with Paul, but the Bible says that those who believe without seeing are blessed.

'Then Jesus told him, "Because you have seen me, you have believed; blessed are those who have not seen and yet have believed."' ***John 20:29 (NIV)***

We need to be prepared to tell unbelievers about Jesus so that they can believe in Him too! This week we are going to learn about different ways that God wants to use us for His glory. I pray that the Holy Spirit will continuously remind you of God's never-ending love, especially during these five days, so that you will have a renewed desire for witnessing to the lost, and for them to know His love as well.

"BUT I HAVE RAISED YOU UP FOR THIS VERY PURPOSE, THAT I MIGHT SHOW YOU MY POWER AND THAT MY NAME MIGHT BE PROCLAIMED IN ALL THE EARTH."
~ EXODUS 9:16 ~

DAY 11 - LOVE

MAIN POINT

The entire earthly life of Jesus was based on love. We see it in every aspect of His human existence from beginning to end. Out of all the instructions to live by, one of the clearest is love. I pray that as we delve into God's word for insight on this subject, that we will have receptive hearts and minds to see His truth, even if it means that we need to work harder to show the love of Jesus to others.

SCRIPTURE

"For you know the grace of our Lord Jesus Christ, that though he was rich, yet for your sake he became poor, so that you through his poverty might become rich." **2 Corinthians 8:9 (NIV)**

The above verse shows that Jesus was sat in Heaven at the right hand of God the Father. Yet He knew that the only way to save us was to leave Heaven and come here to be a servant and die a torturous death to save us from Hell. He wasn't born into royalty and wealth; He was born in a manger to a woman that had no wealth. She simply said yes when God asked her to trust Him. The part of the verse that says "for your sake" means that He did it solely for us, out of love so that we can have fellowship with God.

I don't know very many people that would leave the comfort and security of prosperity and wealth to become poor and considered "less than" so that someone else might experience something good. Especially knowing that the very people that they sacrificed for would laugh at, beat, and crucify them. Jesus knew everything that He would endure and still chose to come and save us. His love trumped all.

We are born with a sinful nature and therefore destined to an eternity of fire and gnashing of teeth. He came to save us from ourselves and when He ascended to Heaven after His resurrection, He left us with a newfound hope and an example of how to live, in order to be right with God the Father.

Read John 13:1-17.

Jesus had already predicted His own death. He was headed toward the end of His earthly ministry and was fully aware that He was about to be betrayed by one of His own disciples. Yet once again, Jesus took on the role of a servant and washed ALL the disciple's feet. This was not a prestigious job. This was a lowly, dirty, and smelly job. And Judas was still part of the group at this point. So, Jesus chose to show love even to the one that He already knew would hand Him over to those that would kill Him.

"You call me 'Teacher' and 'Lord,' and rightly so, for that is what I am. "Now that I, your Lord and Teacher, have washed your feet, you also should wash one another's feet. I have set you an example that you should do as I have done for you. Very truly I tell you, no servant is greater than his master, nor is a messenger greater than the one who sent him. ***John 13:13-16 NIV***

He is giving us instructions here that if the Savior of the World can show unconditional love, forgiveness, and humility, then certainly we should do so. We have no authority; He has been given authority over all of Heaven and Earth by His Father in Heaven. (Matthew 28:18) Jesus should be praised and called Holy, not be in a position of servitude. And yet, He chose to be because He loved us. These next verses are a clear indication of what Jesus says is important and we see a glimpse of the heart that Children of God should have.

1 John 4:7-8 (ESV) *"Beloved, let us love one another, for love is from God, and whoever loves has been born of God and knows God. Anyone who does not love does not know God, because God is love."*

Matthew 22:37-39 (ESV) "And he said to him, "You shall love the Lord your God with all your heart and with all your soul and with all your mind. This is the great and first commandment. And a second is like it: You shall love your neighbor as yourself."

These aren't just suggestions. These are commands! LOVE GOD FIRST AND LOVE PEOPLE SECOND.

I love this next verse from 1 Corinthians. It tells us that we can do all the good works that we want, but if we don't do them out of love, then it means nothing.

1 Corinthians 13:1-7 (NIV) *"If I speak in the tongues of men or of angels, but do not have love, I am only a resounding gong or a clanging cymbal. If I have the gift of prophecy and can fathom all mysteries and all knowledge, and if I have a faith that can move mountains, but do not have love, I am nothing. If I give all I possess to the poor and give over my body to hardship that I may boast, but do not have love, I gain nothing. Love is patient and kind; it does not envy, it does not boast, it is not proud. It does not dishonor others, it is not self-seeking. It is not easily angered, it keeps no record of wrongs. Love does not delight in evil but rejoices with the truth. It always protects, always trusts, always hopes, always perseveres."*

Jesus taught love. Everywhere He went, He showed love and acceptance. He didn't shy away from talking about sin, but He chose to hate the sin, while loving the sinner.

God wants us to follow the example of Jesus. He is the head of the church, the Savior of our souls, and He encountered the same obstacles in life that we do, only He never gave in to the temptations of the world. He was fully human, went through hunger and thirst, happiness and sadness, and joy and grief. He was mocked and ridiculed for who He was and How He spoke, and yet He remained Holy.

How many times in our own lives do people make fun of how we look, talk, or where we come from? How often are Christians called out or left out because of who we are and what we stand for? Jesus went through all of that as well. He endured hardship and strife, was beaten and killed, and yet never wavered in His love or faith in the Father.

The very people that tortured and killed Him are the same people that He came to die for. He never called down the angels to help Him and let's be real, Jesus Christ is part of the Holy Trinity. He could have very easily taken Himself down off that cross. But He loved us so much and knew that dying for us was the only way to save us.

LIFE APPLICATION

We sit in church on Sundays, sing the songs and say the prayers, but do we realize what we are singing and praying about? Do we understand that Jesus loves us even though we spat on Him? Can we see that He have all of Himself to those who would harm Him? Even now, 2,000 years later, He still loves us and forgives us for the things we do wrong. He never tires of us! He never gives up or leaves us! He still stands between us and God, claiming us as His own, even though the world seems to be straying farther and farther from what He taught.

WHAT AN AMAZING LOVE!

God doesn't need us! God wants us! If we were never created, God would still be God and would still control everything. But He wanted our love. He desires a relationship with us.

Are we showing His love not only in our relationship with Him, but in how we treat others? Friend or foe, Jesus loved everyone. Shouldn't we?

PRAYER

Lord, this week I pray that you will open our eyes to see where and to whom we need to show more love. Teach us how to show patience to those that mean to betray us, and how to love them through it. Give us a servant's heart to give even when we will not receive in return. Help us to be more like Jesus. Amen.

"IF YOU LOVE THOSE WHO LOVE YOU, WHAT CREDIT IS THAT TO YOU? FOR EVEN SINNERS LOVE THOSE WHO LOVE THEM. AND IF YOU DO GOOD TO THOSE WHO DO GOOD TO YOU, WHAT CREDIT IS THAT TO YOU? FOR EVEN SINNERS DO THE SAME."

~ JESUS CHRIST ~

DAY 12 - SPREAD THE WORD

Imagine that you are in a desert. There are people everywhere and they are all dying of thirst. Some of them are people you know and love, people that you have spent time with and that you know well. Others are just acquaintances that you have seen around, and the rest are strangers to you. Now imagine that while searching for water, you find a magical river that never ends. It is amazing! The water is clear and clean. Your mouth is watering just thinking about drinking it.

You drink directly from it and immediately you feel refreshed and like new again. This is special water, you realize. Water that keeps you from ever getting thirsty again. Now what do you do? Do you run back to where your family and close friends are and tell them? They are really thirsty, and they could die at any point. They have started getting weighed down and exhausted. They can hardly move at all. All that you need to do, is get them there and let them drink.

So, you run back and tell them, but because they are so weak from dehydration, they can't do it on their own. You must help them get there. You lift them up and help them walk until they can get there because you know that when they finally drink, they will suffer no more. Everything will be alright.

You can't live without these people; they are important to you. You must take several trips back and forth to get everyone there, but they are finally there, now it is up to them. You led them there, but you cannot forcibly make them drink the water. They could just spit it out. What if they don't want the water or think it will run out eventually and we will die later? What if they think that they don't need this water to live? Maybe you should tell them about how the water has quenched your thirst and made you feel like you can never be thirsty again. Maybe they will believe if they see how much better you feel. Maybe that will be proof enough for them. Some of them decide to drink and immediately feel the relief that the water provides. You can visibly see how the water is flowing through them and making them feel like new.

The others that didn't drink the water wonder if this is a trick. Is it real? Does this water really make people better? They aren't ready to drink yet, but now they are starting to think harder about the possibilities. Maybe if more people came and drank of the water then everyone would see the truth. That this is not a trick, this water is really changing people into ones that will never thirst again.

All those other people are still looking for water and haven't found any. Maybe I should go back and tell them about this river. I don't want anybody to die because I didn't tell them about this. Can I be brave enough to tell them about how this water is changing people? Or will they think I am crazy and delirious and not believe me? Will they make fun of me or get mad because they think that they can find water in another direction? What do I do?

The water that we know is so life changing is called the Living Water that is provided to us whenever we accept Jesus as our Savior. Once they realize how Jesus has changed you, some will drink without hesitation. They see the proof in you and need no more urging. Others might be more skeptical, but if they see you and hear your truth, they might not accept Him now, but you have planted some seeds for the future. Those strangers...they need to know Him too. Do you go back for them? Do you risk persecution and ridicule to tell them? They don't even know that they are thirsty. So, when they look at you like you are crazy, remember that they are lost, without any hope, and have compassion for them. They don't know what they are missing. It is as if they have blinders on and can't see the proof in front of them yet. They need more seeds planted and then the next Child of God that comes along, may get a little farther with them than you did. But if you don't try, then more than likely they will die an eternal death filled with despair and a parched throat.

I don't know about you, but I don't want anyone to die of thirst when there is a river right in front of them.

"...but whoever drinks the water I give them will never thirst. Indeed, the water I give them will become in them a spirit of water welling up to eternal life."
~ John 4:14 ~

DAY 13 - GROW IN HIM

MAIN POINT

One of the ways that God wants to use us is to grow our relationship with Him so that we can be mature Christians. Yes, mature! Once we are saved, our job is not done. In fact, our job is just beginning. At that point we are "babes" in Christ. We need guidance from people who have been Christians longer and have been discipled to show us what it means to grow.

He doesn't intend for us to stay the way that we are on the day that He saves us. Yes, He welcomed us just as we were regardless of our past sin, but His intention is to make us into a vessel that He can use to do His very important work, and we cannot stay the same to do that.

The Bible says that people will know us by the fruits that we bear. This means that even though we cannot be saved by our own works. Once we are saved God expects us to start doing good works as we grow stronger in Him. The lost will see the changes that are taking place in us and want to know more about this amazing God that has changed us from the inside out.

SCRIPTURE

"By their fruit you will recognize them. Do people pick grapes from thorn bushes, or figs from thistles? Likewise, every good tree bears good fruit, but a bad tree bears bad fruit. A good tree cannot bear bad fruit, and a bad tree cannot bear good fruit. Every tree that

does not bear good fruit is cut down and thrown into the fire. Thus, by their fruit you will recognize them." **Matthew 7:16-20 (NIV)**

The above verse isn't talking about actual grapes. No, it is talking about spiritual fruits, or the works that we do after we are saved by God's grace. The love and gratitude that we have for what Jesus did for us on the cross makes us want to be more like Him, which means following His examples of doing good works and loving others. As we spend more time with God in prayer and in His Word, we learn how to be more like Jesus. This takes dedication and planning, it is not just something that happens, it's something that we must be intentional about. By spending time with Him, we become more like Jesus and therefore our relationship with God grows stronger and stronger.

"For the grace of God has appeared that offers salvation to all people. It teaches us to say "No" to ungodliness and worldly passions, and to live self-controlled, upright and godly lives in this present age." **Titus 2: 11-12 (NIV)**

However, if we are not bearing good fruit, then we need to reevaluate. Are we spending enough time in His Word, in prayer, and have we truly submitted our lives to Him? If not, then these need to be our first courses of action.

"Those who know your name trust in you, for you, Lord, have never forsaken those who seek you." **Psalm 9:10 (NIV)**

Another reason that God wants to grow us spiritually is so that we will fully trust Him. He always keeps His promises, so if He says it to be true, we'd better put all our eggs in His basket because He will come through.

The life that we live is full of unknowns and what ifs. There is no way to know what will happen tomorrow or if tomorrow will even come. Often, our instincts are to try and handle everything ourselves and try to live without any help from Him, but how is that giving Him any glory? How is that showing Him that we need Him? We must begin to let go of things that keep us from completely surrendering all our trust. The more that we give up our own control and give it to Him, the more that we realize we never had any control to begin with. We only thought that we did.

He shows us that He is the One that we can trust beyond all others. Give up your sin and become more Christlike. Ask Him to help you have strength to battle against your sinful nature. This will continuously remind you of His grace and mercy when you go to Him for forgiveness, and therefore confirming your need and His goodness.

LIFE APPLICATION

In 2010, I thought that I had this mom thing under control. I thought that by having one kid already and he was turning out okay that it meant I knew what I was doing. But I was wrong. When my middle child was five weeks old, he developed a virus that I had never heard of before. One that stopped his breathing and filled his lungs with fluid. He couldn't catch his breath and was making horrible painful noises. And there I was oblivious to it all. I thought he simply had a cold that would go away on its own. Fortunately, my mom had come by to visit and realized what was happening. I still couldn't believe it. I said, "Are you sure? That's crazy! These things don't happen! I just took him to the doctor this morning and they said that he is fine." But we decided that it wouldn't hurt anything to go ahead and have him checked out again.

I have never had a quicker emergency room visit. We walked in, explained the symptoms, and were whisked back to a room where they ended up having to put a tube down his throat to help my baby boy breathe. His body was having to work too hard to take in air, and they had to put him into a medically induced coma, so that they could have machines breathe for him while waiting for his lungs to heal from this virus. At this point, I was freaking out, because I didn't see something right in front of me. I had been prideful and thought I knew what I was doing. He ended up being brought out of the coma a week later and came home a week after that. Thankfully, this story had a happy ending and he still loves to hear this story of his "medical emergency."

While, I don't think that it was my pride that made my child sick, I can see now how God used that circumstance to remind me that I am not in control. He reminded me that at any moment, the life that I think I am "in charge of" can flip upside down. And, it can happen to any of us. He was showing me that in ALL things, I need to be humble and accept help. Whether good or bad, first child or tenth, life or death, I need to recognize my need for Him in all situations. He wants to be there for me, guiding me through life, not sitting on the sidelines while I do it my own way. His intent was for me to ask Him for peace and help. I must allow Him to let His Holy Spirit pour over me and depend on Him in the good as well as the bad.

Sometimes as humans, when we let our pride get in the way of us seeing clearly, and it can cause devastation. We want to think that we are okay, and don't need help but we need to remember that God wants all of us, not just the parts that we are willing to give. He doesn't want to be our "in case of emergency". He wants to be our first stop for help.

So, by putting Him first, trusting Him, and spending more time with Him, He grows us into the women that He intended for us to be. Godly women that don't look to themselves for help, but to Him who can make all things right.

Let Him be above all things that vie for your attention. Immerse yourself in His Word and in prayer, asking for Him to grow your relationship to be more intimate than ever before. Ask him for wisdom and courage in how to talk to other people about your faith, so that they too can know His great and endless love.

God loves us and wants a relationship with us. That's the bottom line. He didn't save us from our sins only to never hear from us again. He saved us from our sins, so that we can be nearer to Him than ever before.

PRAYER

Heavenly Father, we are so amazed by your plan for us. You have the entire puzzle complete while we are still sorting the pieces. Help us to let go of the worldly thoughts that we are in control. Teach us to surrender our needs, wants, fears, and insecurities to You and let You have Your way. And when we pick those worries back up again, be there to guide us back to the cross where we lie them at Jesus' feet once again. Thank you for your love, and for sacrificing the life of Your Son so that we can fellowship with You. We love You Lord! Amen.

"He has saved us and called us to a holy life—not because of anything we have done but because of his own purpose and grace. This grace was given us in Christ Jesus before the beginning of time."

~ 2 Timothy 1:9 ~

DAY 14 - LISTEN

MAIN POINT

Have you ever been around someone who didn't really listen to what you were saying because they are so busy preparing what they will say next? I have and it can be frustrating. Often when people come to us for advice, they just want to be heard. We don't need to say the right thing or to fix it. They just need to get the burdens off their hearts and say it out loud. They don't expect you to know all the answers, but as a friend, they do need you to hear their struggle and empathize with their pain.

SCRIPTURE

Let's dig into Scripture to get an idea about how to better show our love for people through listening rather than speaking.

1 John 3:18 "Dear children, let us not love with words or speech but with actions and in truth."

James 1:19-20 "My dear brothers and sisters, take note of this: Everyone should be quick to listen, slow to speak and slow to become angry, because human anger does not produce the righteousness that God desires."

It is important to take a moment to process our thoughts before speaking, especially when we offended or hurt. You know what I mean. Those times that if you open your mouth and let words fly out before thinking, you will end up biting someone's head off? Our instincts when we've been wounded is to react in anger or retaliation. But, when we do that, we are responding with our emotions rather than letting the Holy Spirit guide us in love.

Maybe God wants that person to see your reaction to what they did in order to gently correct them. Or maybe if you give a forgiving response, they will wonder about the source of your peace and an opportunity to tell them about Jesus will be placed before you. When we respond in anger, it only stirs up more anger.

When I was in high school, I remember responding to my mother with anger…a lot. It seemed like all that we did was butt heads. She wanted what was best for me out of love and I wanted to make my own way in the world. I thought I didn't need to be told what to do. If I would have taken the time to listen to her guidance, rather than storm off and slam a door, I wonder if I would have been less likely to make poor choices later on because I had taken what she had said to heart.

"A gentle answer turns away wrath, but a harsh word stirs up anger." ***Proverbs 15:1 (NIV)***

If you decided to show forgiveness and mercy rather than bitterness to someone that wronged you, how do you think they would react? Do you think that would stop them in their tracks and make them think about what they are doing? More than likely, it would make them hesitate, because kindness and forgiveness are so rare in this world of selfish ambition that they would stop and take notice because it is the opposite of what they expected to receive from you.

But what if they don't stop? What should I do then?

"That is why, for Christ's sake, I delight in weaknesses, in insults, in hardships, in persecutions, in difficulties. For when I am weak, then I am strong." ***2 Corinthians 12:10 (NIV)***

Did that say that I should be joyful when facing insults and difficulties? How is that going to help?

When we go to God for help, it shows our weaknesses at the very moment that we ask for His Power. We are learning to rely on Him and His promises more than what is happening around us. These hard circumstances allow us to grow closer to Him and that is something to celebrate!

"You have heard that it was said, 'Eye for eye, and tooth for tooth.' But I tell you, do not resist an evil person. If anyone slaps you on the right cheek, turn to them the other cheek also. And if anyone wants to sue you and take your shirt, hand over your coat as well. **Matthew 5:38-40 (NIV)**

PRAYER

Heavenly Father, today as we have opened your Word to glean insight on how we can better serve You, we see the need to listen. We realize that we are all guilty at one point or another of rushing to speak before we have fully thought our responses through. We pray for a renewed sense of self-control so that when we are in conversation with those that are hurting, we can properly show our love and understanding. When we find ourselves in a place of disappointment or hurt because of the words of others, please give us strength to consider our words before retaliating in anger or revenge. Lord, we ask these things in Your Son's Precious Name. Amen

"MOST PEOPLE DO NOT LISTEN WITH THE INTENT TO UNDERSTAND; THEY LISTEN WITH THE INTENT TO REPLY."

~ STEPHEN R. COVEY ~

DAY 15 - BUILD UP

MAIN POINT

This week we have been learning about ways that God wants to use us to do His work. Today we will find out about building others up and encouraging them in their walk with the Lord. As we have seen, Jesus is the standard by which we are called to live. Let's once again go to the Word of God to find an example of how we should be that source of love to others.

SCRIPTURE

Read Acts 9:26-31.

At this time in Scripture, Saul (also called Paul) has had his face to face encounter with Jesus. He has truly become a follower of Christ, but considering his previous hatred toward Christians, the other disciples were very hesitant to accept Saul as one of their own. Only one of them was willing to step up and be the friend that Paul needed. Barnabas (meaning Son of Encouragement) took Saul in and vouched for him in front of the other apostles. He told them about Saul's experience with the Lord and how he had already begun preaching in the name of Jesus. Saul was then accepted and began witnessing boldly for Jesus and the church began to grow in numbers.

LIFE APPLICATION

It is very easy for us to go about our daily grind so focused on our own lives that we don't see when someone else needs an uplifting word. In this instance, Paul had just seen the truth about our Lord Jesus Christ. He was a believer. No longer would he persecute Christians. His journey with the Lord was beginning and He was sold out! But if Barnabas had not chosen to befriend and encourage Paul, who knows what would have been the outcome. Clearly Jesus had a plan for Paul to begin his ministry, and thankfully Barnabas stepped up when it seemed as though no one else would.

This is just one example of when Barnabas was an uplifting friend to followers of Jesus. He was known throughout his ministry to always give a positive word and have a supportive spirit. Barnabas was not known as being one of the best writers or bold speakers like Paul or Peter, but if he wouldn't have taken the role that he did, those outspoken leaders of the Christian faith might not have had as much fire in their hearts as they did. We all need people in our lives that are quick give a positive word when we need it.

Do you have friends like that? Friends that will pray for you when you are discouraged, vouch for you, or stay beside you lifting your spirits and supporting you in your work for the Lord?

Also, are we returning the favor? It's not just the people that have a gift for this that should be supportive to other believers. We all should open ourselves up to be this person for someone else. They might not have anyone to tell them good job or lend a word of advice. We all need to hear that we are doing a on the right track and to stand firm.

Are we paying attention when someone needs to have a cheerleader telling them not to give up? Are we seeing the heart of that friend who just needs prayer and to cry on our shoulder? What can we do to build each other up in the Lord so that our boat of life doesn't get overtaken by the constant waves that come our way?

Take some time today and ask people how they are and truly listen to the response. Do you know someone who is trying to find God's purpose or plan for their life, and they need you to pray with them or for them? Do you see a girl in the lunchroom sitting alone who looks like she needs a friend? Be that friend. Say that prayer. Listen to them. You might not always have the "right" answer, but just being there when they need someone is often better than trying to "fix" all their problems.

PRAYER

Lord, today we pray that You will help us to see when and where You want to use us to build up and encourage other people. We know that sometimes You call us to be there for people that we know will not be there for us. But we are confident that You are working in our lives and that person's life. All we can do is be obedient. Show us the way to love others through their happy times and their trying times. Teach us to care about their struggles and empathize with their pain even when we don't understand. Thank You that we can always come to You for help and guidance no matter our struggle and that You never turn us away. Help us to show that love to those that cross our path. In the name of Jesus, Amen.

WEEK 4 - THE WHY

WHY DOES HE WANT TO USE ME?

This is going to be shocking, so prepare yourself... God does not need me. He does not need you. He did not need Adam and Eve and He does not need anything. God is self-sufficient, independent, and not needy for our affection in the least. he is self-sustaining, perfect, all powerful, and creator of all. There has never been a time when He has needed us.

He didn't create us because He needed us, He created us because He wanted us. There is a difference. He wanted our worship and our praise. He wanted to us to enjoy the planet that He created for us and to be good stewards of it. He wanted us to live a life dedicated to Him and His purpose for us. So, it is not about us, it is always about Him. Bottom line: We were created by Him and for Him. So whatever task that He asks of us, we should be eager to complete in order to please our Creator.

The world says that we should do what makes us happy. But the Bible says that we should do what makes God happy. Let's go forward with the intention of pleasing the One that loves us rather than the enemy that wants to destroy us.

He has work for me to do. He has a purpose for my life, and it involves as many people coming to Christ as possible. Our mission is to do Jesus' work that He started during His earthly ministry. I have a purpose. I have a destination. I have a reward.

"God specifically created us to be like Him. This is impossible to wrap our minds around, but God created us like Him in some respect and then set us in the midst of this world to represent Him!"
~ Francis Chan ~

DAY 16 - HANDS & FEET

MAIN POINT

We know that Jesus is our example of how to live. We are to strive to be more like Him, and that is exactly what it means to be the hands and feet of Jesus. It means to do His work while we are here on Earth. Before He ascended back up into Heaven to sit at the right hand of God the Father, Jesus gave instructions to the disciples that were witnessing this, but also to all of us that desire to be more like Him.

Let's see what the Bible says about this.

SCRIPTURE

1 John 2:6 "Whoever claims to live in Him must live as Jesus did."

John 14:12 "Very truly I tell you, whoever believes in me will do the works I have been doing, and they will do even greater things than these, because I am going to the Father."

Let's think of a few ways that we can live like Jesus:

- Help those in need – Jesus was constantly helping people wherever He went. Whether they were sick, paralyzed, demon possessed, poor, lonely, or just lost.

- While we cannot physically heal people, we can help take care of those who can't take care of themselves. We can be a shoulder for them to lean on and an ear to the lonely.

- We can donate food to the poor or just raise awareness of the growing problem of hunger.

- We can visit the lonely or mow the grass of someone who cannot physically get out and do it.

- We can collect baby diapers and clothing for moms who cannot afford them, or book bags and school supplies for kids whose parents can't buy them.

"But if anyone has the material possessions and sees a brother or sister in need, but has no pity on them, how can the love of God be in that person?" ***1 John 3:17 (NIV)***

- Love the unlovable – Jesus loved those that were unwanted and alone, and He still does even now. He was the first person to go to the excluded or the unloved and show them kindness. If you see that girl at school that no one wants to eat with, or that walks alone to class every day, pull up a chair and join her or walk to class with her. Let people see that you care about them. It can help them feel self-worth and value when they think someone cares about them. What about the girl that has a "bad reputation?" You see people talking badly about her behind her back, why not stand up for her? Tell them that we all make bad choices sometimes, but we shouldn't allow it to cause us to be judgmental. Tomorrow it could be you, and wouldn't you want someone to take up for you? Often, all it takes is one person to stand up and others will follow.

"But to you who are listening I say: Love your enemies, do good to those who hate you, bless those who curse you, pray for those who

mistreat you. If someone slaps you on one cheek, turn to them the other also. If someone takes your coat, do not withhold your shirt from them. Give to everyone who asks you, and if anyone takes what belongs to you, do not demand it back. Do to others as you would have them do to you." ***Luke 6:27-31 (NIV)***

- Forgive them – Forgive those who have wronged you. Even as Jesus hung on the cross, in pain and misery, he said "Father forgive them, they know not what they do"

"Hatred stirs up conflict, but love covers over all wrongs." ***Proverbs 10:12 (NIV)***

The people that had beaten Him and hung Him on that cross didn't ask for forgiveness or even realize that they needed it. But here Jesus was, offering forgiveness even as He hung there in pain.

Whether someone has wronged you and apologized, or still think that they have nothing to be sorry about, it is better for us if we forgive them. The reality is that even our worst enemy, the person that we like the least in all the world still needs Jesus. No matter how much that person has hurt me, I must let it go and forgive. Not only for them, but if we hold on to all that bitterness and let it affect the way that we see things, it can cause us to stumble in our quest to be more Christlike.

That person doesn't know and will never know that we have chosen to let it go. It is not for them that we forgive, it is for our Father in Heaven who wants all of me. Not just the parts that we are ready to give, but all of us. He calls us to lay down our grudges and let Him take over all of it. How can we say that we love Jesus but hate our brother?

"Anyone who claims to be in the light but hates a brother or sister is still in the darkness." ***1 John 2:9 (NIV)***

We must forgive. Even when forgiving means that the person will never know the extent of my pain, and even though the other person is wrong.

There are times in my life when I have hurt someone. I hope that they will forgive me as well. Let's let go of our burdens, our anger, our bitterness, and seek Him wholeheartedly holding nothing back. Let's give Him all of us. So, let's decide to love, above all things. Love people like he did, whether they are kind or not, welcoming or not, Christian or lost, hate me or love me. It doesn't matter, I am called to love them. After all, God loves me no matter what I have done, shouldn't I show the same love to others?

"Bear with each other and forgive one another if any of you has a grievance against someone. Forgive as the Lord forgave you." ***Colossians 3:13 (NIV)***

- Look Around - In every situation, keep your head up and look around for the lost. Pay attention to what people need so that you can know how to share Jesus with them. Tell them about how Jesus has changed your life and why you needed Him to. This is our most important job as Christians. Even if they don't accept Him today, the seeds have been planted and maybe the next time they hear the Gospel, they will.

"Therefore go and make disciples of all nations, baptizing them in the name of the Father and of the Son and of the Holy Spirit." ***Matthew 28:19 (NIV)***

- Pray for people – What better way to serve others than to pray for them regularly. If there is someone that you know is lost, pray for their heart to be softened and their eyes to be opened to the truth of His Word. Pray for God to work in health situations and to show his awesome and mighty power.

"Therefore, confess your sins to each other and pray for each other so that you may be healed. The prayer of a righteous person is powerful and effective." ***James 5:16 (NIV)***

- Serve – Everywhere Jesus went, he was teaching others about God. Are you involved in a church? If so, ask if there are ways that you can help teach younger children about Jesus. Get involved in the youth group and serve alongside of people your age. Give back to your community with your time and energy. Donate to ministries in need in your area. Pray for God to show you areas that He wants to expand your personal mission field. Ask Him for guidance on where to start and for Him to make your desires match His.

Jesus came to Earth and lived sin free and then died for us so that we can have eternal life. We, however, will never live up to that. We sin daily and don't deserve anything other than eternal separation from God. But praise Jesus that we don't have to live with that punishment. Even though we can't hope to be perfect on this side of Heaven, we can live our lives as a daily sacrifice to He who is.

PRAYER

Dear Lord, how humbling it is when we think about what You have done for us. You love us so much and yet we don't deserve it and still screw up every single day. Thank you for loving us regardless of our past. Thank you for planning a future for us that includes spending eternity with You. We pray today that You will clearly show us where You intend for us to be Your Hands and Feet. Teach us to give to others, even if it means that we ourselves might not have something. Remind us daily of Your sacrifice so that we can go out and sacrifice ourselves for You. In Jesus name I pray, Amen.

"GOD IS NOT CALLING US TO GO TO CHURCH; HE IS CALLING US TO BE HIS CHURCH."
~ CRAIG GROESCHEL ~

DAY 17 - STAND OUT

MAIN POINT

It is so easy to follow instead of lead. Satan wants us to blend in with the rest of the world when we were made to stand out. Do not go along with the crowd just because you don't want to be made fun of. You are a child of God! You have been set apart and chosen by Him to tell others about His love. Don't let fear of being different keep you from being who He designed you to be.

If they make fun of you or say that you are weird or a Jesus freak, Praise God for that! That means you are different and unique! That means you aren't going along with what the world says just because it is a popular thing to do. It means that you are stepping out on faith and trusting that He will give you the words to say when you need them. You are showing the world who you belong to, and that you will not give in to things that you know are not right in your Creator's eyes. I cannot think of a better freak to be than one that loves Jesus more than anything else.

SCRIPTURE

"Do not conform to the pattern of this world, but be transformed by the renewing of your mind. Then you will be able to test and approve what God's will is – his good, pleasing and perfect will." ***Romans 12:2 (NIV)***

Conforming to the world means to adopt the ways of or become like the world. As Christians, we should let the Holy Spirit guide us in telling that is of the Will of God and what is not. We should not go along with what other people say is right or wrong. The Bible is our Word of Truth and our compass. In order to know whether we are doing right all we must do is open it and read.

"Do not love the world or anything in the world. If anyone loves the world, love for the Father is not in them. For everything in the world—the lust of the flesh, the lust of the eyes, and the pride of life—comes not from the Father but from the world. The world and its desires pass away, but whoever does the will of God lives forever." ***1 John 2:15-17 (NIV)***

BE DIFFERENT! You are not like everyone else in the world. You are different and set apart for a purpose that is greater than yourself. You were made to stand up and speak out on His behalf. Not to let others tell you who He is. He is your Savior and King and your number one priority. The reason that you wake up every morning and the reason that you have peace about your future.

PRAYER

Lord, show us the path to righteousness. Remind us each day that we do not belong here, that this world is a temporary place for us to stay while we wait for Your return. Though we are constantly bombarded by the temptations of this world, strengthen our faith so that we can do Your work while we are here and not be distracted by the enemy. In Jesus' Name I pray, Amen.

DAY 18 - BE COURAGEOUS

MAIN POINT

A couple of years ago I felt God leading me away from a ministry that I had been in for a long time. I was hesitant because this was my comfort zone and where I felt the most confident. I knew that God had other plans for me, but at that time all I knew was that I needed to be obedient. Throughout this process, I was asked repeatedly if I was sure that this is what God had planned for me and if I could be talked out of it. I found myself fully convinced of the path that God was leading me to, but my discernment was being questioned.

I had to make a choice. Would I stand firm in what my Lord was calling me to do regardless of what other people thought? Would I back away in fear of making waves and dealing with people who clearly didn't understand?

I chose to stand rooted in the instruction from my Lord and since that time, He has continued to show me that He wanted to draw me closer to Himself. He wanted me to trust Him in the little things so that when the big things came my way, my gaze wouldn't stray from His.

When you become a child of the God, He will call you to stay rooted in Him while the world is constantly saying that He is wrong. He will ask you to come out of your comfort zone and do things that are intimidating. In these situations, it is normal to be afraid. It's hard to share your faith for fear of being made fun of or making people angry, but He calls us to righteousness through His power. We must be courageous and have peace in His plan regardless of what everybody else is doing and saying.

The lost of this world need to know that there is a better way, a way to avoid separation from God in Hell, and a way to live life with the joy and peace that He offers all of us. They need to know that Jesus is their Savior, and it can take a lot of courage to tell people about Him!

2 Timothy 1:7 "For the Spirit God gave us does not make us timid, but gives us power, love and self-discipline."

Joshua 1:9 "Have I not commanded you? Be strong and courageous. Do not be afraid; do not be discouraged. For the Lord your God will be with you wherever you go."

Today, we are going to look at a woman who used courage to serve the Lord.

SCRIPTURE

ESTHER

It takes a lot of courage to stand up for God when your life is on the line. In this day and age, we worry about offending people and being made fun of, but in the story of Esther, she was facing death if things didn't go well. We are going to see that she feared speaking out, but that ultimately, she put her trust in the Lord and He gave her boldness to help the Jewish people.

In the book of Esther Chapter 2, Esther becomes the new queen. This was after the previous queen had been banished from the king's sight for not coming when he called her. So, she begins her reign on somewhat shaky ground. The last thing that she wanted to do was make the king mad or she could be banished next.

In Verse 19, her uncle Mordecai finds out that Haman had tricked the king into signing a law that would destroy all the Jewish people. It wasn't common knowledge, but Esther was Jewish and therefore when her uncle told her about this, she was scared, but she also wanted to remain in the king's good graces. In those times, there was a strict rule about seeing the king. You must be summoned or else you are subject to death unless the king extends the golden scepter to you. In Chapter 4, Mordecai tried to talk Esther into going to the king to tell him what had happened. Esther realized that this was too serious not to act, and she requested for the Jewish people to pray and fast for three days. After that she would go to the king regardless of the punishment.

She prayed and asked God to take away her fear, and on the third day went to see the king. He did in fact extend the golden scepter to her and the king asked her what she wanted. Later in Chapter 7, Esther explained the situation, and asked that he overrule the previous edict so that the Jewish people would not be destroyed. Once the king realized that he has been tricked by Haman, he complied with her request and then had Haman sentenced to death.

If Esther would have let fear dictate her ways, many Jews could have been killed including her and her family. That is bravery! To stand up and say something when you know that something is wrong even when faced with possible death. That is the kind of Christian that I want to be. FEARFUL in my own abilities but FEARLESS in His!

When you are out in the world, you will see things happening that don't align with God's Word. These things will be made to seem normal and okay. They are not. The Word of God is not optional, it is a requirement for those that love the Lord.

"All Scripture is God-breathed and is useful for teaching, rebuking, correcting and training in righteousness, so that the servant of God may be thoroughly equipped for every good work." ***2 Timothy 3:16-17 (NIV)***

I am not saying that we should go around condemning these people to Hell. The opposite in fact, Jesus proclaimed the truth in a loving way. He wasn't on a high horse talking down to sinners, He took the role of a servant and spoke with humility and love. When someone questioned Him, He didn't verbally or physically attack them, he merely explained what the truth is without worrying about what people would say about Him. We cannot force people to make the right choices, but we can educate them and show them the love of Christ while praying that the Lord will continue to soften their hearts and make them receptive.

Fear is a normal emotion. We are all afraid of something. The part that we have a choice in is are we going to trust God to provide courage to fight the enemy, or will we wallow in our fears and stay quiet?

PRAYER

Father, thank You for Your Son's perfect example of how we should live. Thank You for loving us enough to send Him to save us. We pray that when we are out in the world, that You would give us the right words to say to those that question our faith. Help us to show people that You are love and truth, but that we would do so in a way that people can see You in us. Give us courage to stand up when we know something is wrong. Teach us not to fear anything to decide to follow You no matter the cost. In the name of Jesus, Amen.

"FEAR IS A REACTION. COURAGE IS A DECISION."
~ SIR WINSTON CHURCHILL ~

DAY 19 - BE AN EXAMPLE

MAIN POINT

One day as I was running around the house putting things in their place, washing clothes, helping with homework, and fixing dinner, I heard my daughter's voice in another room. I walked slowly around the corner to find her "talking" to her friends on her Barbie phone. She had the phone propped between her shoulder and her cheek and explaining to the imaginary voice on the other end of the line all the things that she needed to do today. Between the "oh my!" and the "Are you serious?" she put one hand on her hip and with attitude yelled over her shoulder, "EVERYBODY BEHAVE! I AM ON THE PHONE!"

After I finished laughing myself silly realizing that she was pretending to be me, I thought about how often I am being watched without even realizing it. My children are little sponges soaking up my reactions to the good, the bad, and the ugly. They see the real me. The parts that aren't on display for the rest of the world to see. Am I being the example of a Christian woman that I wanted my daughter to emulate and my sons to look for in a wife one day? Am I practicing what I was preaching in teaching them Godly ways while at the same time living them out?

This is not only a question that affects my children, it could transfer to all aspects of life.

Am I an ambassador for Christ in the pew on Sunday only, or can my friends see Him in me on Saturday nights too?

In Wal-Mart if someone goes ahead of me in line, do I question their audacity and pitch a fit or show them kindness and be five minutes late?

Do I yell at people or call them names because of their sin, or do I show them the love of Jesus and tell them how to know Him too?

SCRIPTURE

Let's find some Biblical examples to show that setting an example is what God expects of us.

"Whoever says he abides in him ought to walk in the same way in which he walked." ***1 John 2:6 (ESV)***

"Let no one despise you for your youth, but set the believers an example in speech, in conduct, in love, in faith, in purity." ***1 Timothy 4:12 (ESV)***

"For to this you have been called, because Christ also suffered for you, leaving you an example, so that you might follow in his steps." ***1 Peter 2:21 (ESV)***

"Be imitators of me, as I am of Christ." ***1 Corinthians 11:1 (ESV)***

"Show yourself in all respects to be a model of good works, and in your teaching show integrity, dignity..." ***Titus 2:7 (ESV)***

"In the same way, let your light shine before others, so that they may see your good works and give glory to your Father who is in heaven." ***Matthew 5:16 (ESV)***

I am not saying that we are going to be perfect. We are sinners and as such, we will mess up. But if we are being watched by others, Christians and non-Christians alike, what are they seeing when they look at us? Do they even know that I am a Christian or would they be surprised to find out? Are they seeing me feel shame when I sin or do I even react at all anymore?

Jesus came to Earth to die for us, but He also showed us a perfect example of Godliness. He also gave us a purpose to "Go and make disciples of all the nations..." Matthew 28:19-20. Yes, we need to share the Gospel with people, but we also need to show the Gospel to them.

PRAYER

Dear Lord, thank you for showing us how important it is that we tell others about Jesus by how we live. We pray that as we go about our daily lives that you will remind us that we are representing You. Help us to be firm and steadfast in doing the right things and standing up for You when we should so that others will see how You change Your children to be more like Yourself. In Jesus' Name I pray, Amen.

DAY 20 - THINK ETERNALLY

MAIN POINT

Have you ever heard the song by Building 429 called, "Not Where I Belong?" The idea of the song is that though we face so many trials and struggles here on Earth, this is not our home. We should never feel like we are part of this world, but that this is an instance in which we want to be on the outside looking in. They say "Take this world and give me Jesus" because even though we live here, even though this is where our physical bodies will be buried, our souls will never be home until we are with Jesus.

When Christians are at the end of our earthly lives, it is not the end, but the beginning. The beginning of an eternity spent with our Savior, singing songs of praise and worshiping at His feet. We live with this hope every day. No matter what happens to us here on Earth, we have HOPE that there is a brighter tomorrow and we should live our lives with this in mind.

We have received instructions from Jesus about our work here. Jesus said that we should love the Lord, love others, and make disciples. These are tasks that we can accomplish for Him here that will affect our eternity. We will receive treasures in Heaven based on the work that we do for Jesus here.

When Jesus saved Me, He changed me. No longer do I only think about what is happening today. Now I can see that the choices I make can either increase my ability to do those tasks or hurt them. For example, if I live my life only for today and never do God's work, then how am I loving Him and making Him my first priority? If I constantly put myself first and do what I want all the time, I am not loving others as I should. And how can I make disciples if I am not being a good disciple myself?

This life is but a whisper in the wind. We will all look up one day and wonder where the time went, because it flies so quickly. Did we do everything that we could, in the time given, to make sure that we helped as many people as possible come to know Jesus? Or did I live for myself and not do much to grow the Kingdom of God. Let's make the choice to STORE UP TREASURES in heaven rather than collecting worldly things that we can't take with us anyways.

SCRIPTURE

"So, we fix our eyes not on what is seen, but on what is unseen, since what is seen is temporary, but what is unseen is eternal." ***2 Corinthians 4:18 (NIV)***

Paul is saying that we should focus on the eternal because the things of this world, including all our troubles, disappointments, and failures are only temporary.

"Set your mind on the things above, not on earthly things." ***Colossians 3:2 (NIV)***

"For we must all appear before the judgment seat of Christ, so that each of us may receive what is due us for the things done while in the body, whether good or bad." ***2 Corinthians 5:10 (NIV)***

We will all answer for the Heavenly work or lack thereof that was done on Earth.

"Jesus turned and said to Peter, "Get behind me, Satan! You are a stumbling block to me; you do not have in mind the concerns of God, but merely human concerns." ***Matthew 16:23 (NIV)***

The enemy wants us to think only of ourselves. He doesn't want us doing work for the Lord, because that would mean that more people are coming to Jesus. He wants us as far away from Jesus as possible. He wants us thinking of what we want in the moment rather than what the Lord wants for us. The darkness of this world makes "what feels good" more important than what the Lord has planned.

He has a vision for us that we cannot begin to fathom. It is a life of servitude to Him, yes, but also a life of joy and peace. These things might not seem important in this world of wealth and security, but if we look past all of the shiny cars and new I-phones, we can see that the most fulfilling life to live is one that is spent in complete surrender to the One that made us and saved us. This is the life spent building others up in the faith of the Lord rather than focusing on what this world has to offer in the here and now. The devil is crafty and puts the very things that are likely to make us stumble in front of us to distract us from our true purpose of accomplishing God's work for us.

We can spend so much time worrying about the desires of the world that we forget that we already have everything we need in HIM. He is everything that we need.

PRAYER

Heavenly Father, we come to You today grateful for the reminder of Your eternal promises. As we are living in a world in which we do not belong, it can be so easy to get distracted by the worldly temptations that the enemy sends our way. Teach us to persevere for You during those temptations. Continue to remind us of the place that You have prepared for us. Guide us in how to tell others about Your great love and sacrifice. You are so awesome Lord, we don't deserve any of the goodness that you have bestowed upon us, but we are so filled with thanks that You give it so freely. Help us to do the work that You have laid out so clearly for us to do to further Your Kingdom. We pray for the souls of all of those that are lost. Draw them closer to Yourself so that when they hear about You from us, they will be more likely to accept Your gift of Salvation. In Jesus' name I pray, Amen.

"MY HOME IS IN HEAVEN. I'M JUST TRAVELING THROUGH THIS WORLD."

~ BILLY GRAHAM ~

WEEK 5 - THE HOW

HOW CAN I BE READY WHEN GOD WANTS TO USE ME?

If our priority is Jesus, and He wants us to bring more people to know Him, then how can we go about doing that? Well I would say that the best thing that we can do is be prepared for any and all opportunities to share the gospel whether through word or deed.

I am a little bit OCD about organizing and preparation. Anyone that knows me well, would tell you that I must have a laid-out step by step plan for things, otherwise I get a little freaked out. It's just that I like to be ready for any and all questions or obstacles that might come my way and I usually have a back-up plan in case my first approach doesn't work. While I would say that this is not always a good quality and drives many people close to me insane, in the case of sharing the gospel, I would rather be prepared than not.

"But in your hearts revere Christ as Lord. Always be prepared to give an answer to everyone who asks you to give the reason for the hope that you have. But do this with gentleness and respect..." ***1 Peter 3:15 (NIV)***

So how can we be prepared to share the Gospel? This week I have laid out five different ways that God can use to prepare not only our heads, but our hearts for when the opportunity arises to tell others about His great love.

- BE IN THE WORD
- PRAY CONSTANTLY

- BE STILL & LISTEN
- CHOOSE INFLUENCES WISELY
- HAVE A WILLING HEART

Most of these are things that we already do, but we are going to learn how they can each help us to be ready to give a reason for our hope in Jesus.

PRAYER

Father, I pray that as we go through our devotions this week, that You would mold our hearts to be more like You. Give us the words to say when we don't have any. Teach us ways that we can improve our relationship with You so that we are more confident than ever in our reasons for hope. Help us to have receptive hearts to listen when You gently show us where to improve. We love You Lord! In Jesus' Name, Amen

"GOD WILL PUT PREPARED PEOPLE IN THE WAY OF HIS PREPARED SERVANTS WHO WANT TO SHARE THE GOSPEL."

~ HENRY B EYRING ~

DAY 21 - THE WORD

MAIN POINT

The Word of God is our life manual. It guides us in the overall way that we should live our lives, if we want to do it in His way. It is God-breathed and holy. We, as children of God are to spend time in the Bible regularly. Not just during the struggles, but through blessings too. The more that we are in the Scriptures and speaking with God through prayer, He begins to take over. We are reading His ways and allowing our minds to be opened to his truths. When you are willing, He will answer. I like to pray before I open my Bible for God to show me the truths that He wants to reveal through our time together. Then I pray after I read, asking Him to grant me strength to be His vessel that day and for me to cast his shining light for all to see.

Today we are going to talk about how the power of the Bible and why it is important that we make reading it a priority.

SCRIPTURE

- HIS WORD IS HOLY

"All Scripture is breathed out by God and profitable for teaching, for reproof, for correction, and for training in righteousness," ***2 Timothy 3:16 (ESV)***

"Therefore, get rid of all moral filth and the evil that is so prevalent and humbly accept the word planted in you, which can save you." ***James 1:21 (NIV)***

- HIS WORD IS TRUTH

"Sanctify them in the truth; your word is truth." **John 17:17 (ESV)**

Every word of God proves true; he is a shield to those who take refuge in him." **Proverbs 30:5 (ESV)**

- HIS WORD IS ALIVE

"For the word of God is living and active, sharper than any two-edged sword, piercing to the division of soul and of spirit, of joints and of marrow, and discerning the thoughts and intentions of the heart." **Hebrews 4:12 (ESV)**

"Since you have been born again, not of perishable seed but of imperishable, through the living and abiding word of God;" **1 Peter 1:23 (ESV)**

- HIS WORD IS ETERNAL

"In the beginning was the Word, and the Word was with God, and the Word was God." **John 1:1 (ESV)**

"The grass withers, the flower fades, but the word of our God will stand forever." **Isaiah 40:8 (ESV)**

"Heaven and earth will pass away, but my words will not pass away." **Matthew 24:35 (ESV)**

- HIS WORD IS CONVICTING

"I seek you with all my heart; do not let me stray from your commands. I have hidden your word in my heart, that I might not sin against you." **Psalm 119:10-11 (NIV)**

"They show that the work of the law is written on their hearts, while their conscience also bears witness, and their conflicting thoughts accuse or even excuse them." ***Romans 2:15 (ESV)***

- HIS WORD IS UNCHANGING

"And if anyone takes away from the words of the book of this prophecy, God will take away his share in the tree of life and in the holy city, which are described in this book." ***Revelation 22:19 (ESV)***

- HIS WORD GUIDES MY STEPS

"Your word is a lamp for my feet, a light on my path." ***Psalm 119:105 (ESV)***

"The unfolding of your words gives light; it imparts understanding to the simple." ***Psalm 119:130 (ESV)***

- HIS WORD IS ENCOURAGING

"Keep this Book of the Law always on your lips; meditate on it day and night, so that you may be careful to do everything written in it. Then you will be prosperous and successful." ***Joshua 1:8 (ESV)***

"But he said, "Blessed rather are those who hear the word of God and keep it!" ***Luke 11:28 (ESV)***

These are just some of the many verses about God's Word. But why should we read the Bible? Apart from the reasons listed in the verses above, if we are Children of God, we should desire to be in His presence and learn more about him. Aside from prayer, this is the best way to be close with Him than to be consistently studying the words that He inspired.

Another good reason to memorize Scripture is so that we can be ready with verses on the tips of our tongues when we are explaining the Gospel to the lost. If people ask us questions, and we don't have answers about the book that we are living our life by, then why would they believe what we say? We cannot memorize the entire Bible obviously, but we can spend time memorizing the verses that will most likely come up when we witness. And people WILL ask. We cannot live on fire for Jesus without people taking notice. HE IS SOUL SAVING AND LIFE CHANGING!! With His Word roaring like a lion inside of us, the Holy Spirit will begin to overflow from our mouths and actions.

Another reason to memorize Scripture is to battle temptation. Satan knows our personal struggles. He is very crafty and is fully aware of what temptation is most likely to cause me to sin. He is our enemy and what he wants most is for us to be separated from our Heavenly Father. When Jesus was in the wilderness and Satan tempted Him, Jesus called on Bible verses to help Him. And it worked! In Matthew 4:1-11, we can see that when Satan couldn't trick Jesus, he left Him and then angels attended to Jesus. Wow! Jesus went through the same temptations that we do, and He chose to use Scripture. Clearly, we should too so that we can fight Satan off. Then when we are in a moment of struggle, we won't have to go look for verses, they will already be hidden in our hearts.

When we don't know the ways of the Lord, it is like we stumble in the darkness trying to feel our way around. But the Holy Bible is a lamp and a light that guides our way in the dark. We don't know the way to live without it. We just roam around going our own way, sinning and causing a separation between us and Him. We need to be in the Light to see the way to righteousness.

Sometimes the Bible is hard to understand. In my own quiet time, I can fly through most of the New Testament, but when I arrive at Revelations, it is like I am trying to see through a window that has not been cleaned in a while. I can make out the overall picture, but the details are very hazy. The Old Testament is my fave. I love to read the accounts of all Moses, the kings and all the prophets, but when I get to the Numbers and Chronicles, I struggle to maintain my focus.

Recently, I was attempting to make it through the entire Old Testament. I made it to Ecclesiastes and then I realized that I was not soaking it in. I was just reading it and not retaining. I couldn't tell you what I had read the night before or even what chapter I was on. At that point, I went back to a book that I could better focus on until I felt ready to come back to Ecclesiastes.

You see, when we don't understand the Word, we have options. We are not supposed to give up and say, "Oh well, that is too hard." Because if we ask God for clarity and guidance, and open our hearts to hear it, He will do it, in His time. So, until that time, we can continue to pray for understanding, but go to a place in scripture that we easily understand. We can read one verse many times and every time gain new insights on it.

After spending time in the Word consistently and praying daily, God will begin changing us. The Holy Spirit inside of us begins to make your thoughts more like His. When that happens, we start to develop a desire to be in the Word more. It is like once you feel the sunlight on your face at the end of a cold winter, you want to see the sun every day. The Holy Spirit increases our desire to learn more, want to be with God more, and please Him in word and deed. When He is the first thought as we wake up and the last thought before we close our eyes, He is becoming our priority, and that is a beautiful thing.

"Let the message of Christ dwell among you richly as you teach and admonish one another with all wisdom through psalms, hymns and songs from the Spirit, singing to God with gratitude in your hearts." **Colossians 3:16 (NIV)**

PRAYER

Father, we thank You for Your Word. Thank You that we can count on You to guide us in it, and that there is not a question that we can ask that we cannot find the answer to in the Scriptures. We need this life manual that You provided to keep us in right standing with You and to remind us of the truth of The Gospel when the days are long, and the obstacles seem impossible. Help us to commit to spending more time in it each day and memorizing parts that will help us to give more glory to You. In Jesus' Name I pray. Amen.

"If you abide in me, and my words abide in you, ask whatever you wish, and it will be done for you."

~ John 15:7 (NASB) ~

DAY 22 - PRAYER

MAIN POINT

When we accept Jesus as our Savior, we are requesting to have a relationship with Him. When we think about our other relationships in life, how do we become closer with them? Probably, by spending time and enjoying things together, am I right?

The same goes for our friendship with Jesus. In order to get to know Him better, we must spend time with Him regularly. This happens during our daily quiet time by reading the Bible, but also through consistent prayer. How can we be close with someone that we don't ever talk to?

"Look to the Lord and His strength; seek His face always." ***1 Chronicles 16:11 (NIV)***

Everyone in my life that I don't talk to regularly, I would consider an acquaintance, while anyone that I spend time with and talk to frequently is usually a close friend. They are the ones that I call when I am in trouble and need help or advice. They are the ones that know our secrets and struggles and cheer us on when we need encouragement. It is the same with our relationship with Jesus. If we desire to be close with Him and yet don't spend time with Him, how can we expect to have an intimacy like we have with our closest confidantes?

Prayer is the number one way for us to communicate with our Lord and Savior. He is always there, waiting for us to come to Him. He wants to help us through hard times and be there to cheer us on in the good times. He doesn't want us to come only when we need help, He wants us to come to Him with everything. When we are making decisions throughout our day, He wants to be the one that helps us with them. He wants to be our all in all, our first call rather than our "in case of emergency."

"Devote yourselves to prayer, being watchful and thankful." ***Colossians 4:2 (NIV)***

SCRIPTURE

Let's look at Scripture to see the account of Hannah.

Read 1 Samuel 1:2 – 2:11.

Hannah was one of two wives to a man named Elkanah. The Lord had closed her womb and therefore she had no children. The other wife had many sons and daughters and chose to constantly provoke Hannah to irritate her.

One year, while they were in Shiloh to worship the Lord, the other wife, Peninnah was being so mean to Hannah that she went to the Temple in tears. She was in anguish because of Peninnah, and because she couldn't have a child. She cried out in prayer to the Lord asking for a child and swearing an oath that if He would allow her to give birth, that she would dedicate the child to be raised in the instruction of the Lord. She poured her soul out that day.

The Lord remembered Hannah and she later became pregnant and gave birth to a son, Samuel. After he was weaned, Hannah took him to the Temple to see Eli the priest. She told him that the Lord had granted her prayer to be a mother and that she was there to dedicate Samuel to the Lord to live and be raised in His ways. So, Samuel stayed with Eli and was raised in the instruction of the Lord. Samuel became a great prophet to the nation of Israel.

LIFE APPLICATION

Have you ever had a situation that grieved you so deeply that you just cried out to God in pain? Those are the times that we might not even have the words to say to express what's happening. But we can take comfort in the promise that God already knows. He knows everything about us. Our fears, our worries, our heartaches, and our joys. Before we even say a word, He is already working on our circumstance. Sometimes it takes a while to see, but He has plans for our good and we just must wait for His timing.

"Even before a word is on my tongue, behold, O Lord, you know it altogether." ***Psalm 139:4 (ESV)***

Hannah prayed to God with a purpose. She made her request known to the Lord and He had compassion on her because He loved her. He allowed her to become pregnant. He has the same love for us. When we pour out our hearts to God, He hears us and if it is part of His plan, He will give us the answer that we request.

I call my best friend several times a week. Sometimes it is for help, but most of the time it is just to chat about what's going on that week or to laugh about something that I know she will get. How much more important is my Savior and Lord? When we are driving down the road or doing laundry we can just stop and say thank you, or I love you. It doesn't have to be a long prayer. It's just about acknowledging His presence and who He is.

I came across this illustration written by Robert Boyd Munger in the book Having a Mary Heart in a Martha World and it spoke volumes to me. I pray that it does for you as well.

'My Heart – Christ's Home "Without question one of the most remarkable Christian doctrines is that Jesus Christ Himself through the presence of the Holy Spirit will actually enter a heart, settle down and be at home there," Munger says. "[Jesus] came into the darkness of my heart and turned on the light. He built a fire in the cold hearth and banished the chill. He started music where there had been stillness and He filled the emptiness with His own loving, wonderful fellowship." Munger goes on to tell how he showed Christ around the house of his heart, inviting him to "settle down and be perfectly at home," welcoming Him room by room.

Together they visited the library of his mind— "a very small room with very thick walls." They peered into the dining room of his appetites and desires. They spent a little time in the workshop where his talents and skills were kept, and the rumpus room of "certain associations and friendships, activities and amusements." They even poked their heads into the hall closet filled with dead, rotting things he had managed to hoard. As Pastor Munger described each room, they reflected my heart as well. But it was his depiction of the drawing room that would forever change the way I viewed my time with the Lord. Especially when I considered the picture of friendship with God he portrayed.

We walked next into the drawing room. This room was rather intimate and comfortable. I liked it. It had a fireplace, overstuffed chairs, a bookcase, sofa, and a quiet atmosphere. He also seemed pleased with it. He said, "This is indeed a delightful room. Let us come here often. It is secluded and quiet and we can have fellowship together." Well, naturally, as a young Christian I was thrilled. I could not think of anything I would rather do than have a few minutes apart with Christ in intimate comradeship.

He promised, "I will be here every morning early. Meet with Me here and we will start the day together." So, morning after morning, I would come downstairs to the drawing room and He would take a book of the Bible…open it and then we would read together. He would tell me of its riches and unfold to me its truths.… They were wonderful hours together. In fact, we called the drawing room the "withdrawing room." It was a period when we had our quiet time together.

But little by little, under the pressure of many responsibilities, this time began to be shortened.… I began to miss a day now and then.… I would miss it two days in a row and often more. I remember one morning when I was in a hurry.… As I passed the drawing room, the door was ajar. Looking in I saw a fire in the fireplace and the Lord sitting there.… "Blessed Master forgive me. Have You been here all these mornings?" "Yes," He said, "I told you I would be here every morning to meet with you." Then I was even more ashamed. He had been faithful in spite of my faithlessness. I asked His forgiveness and

He readily forgave me....He said, "The trouble with you is this: You have been thinking of the quiet time, of the Bible study and prayer time, as a factor in your own spiritual progress, but you have forgotten that this hour means something to Me also."

"Therefore the Lord waits to be gracious to you, and therefore he exalts himself to show mercy to you. For the Lord is a God of justice; blessed are all those who wait for him." ***Isaiah 30:18 (ESV)***

"Call to me and I will answer you and tell you great and unsearchable things you do not know." ***Jeremiah 33:3 (NIV)***

I pray that we will grow in our prayer lives with Jesus and that He will begin a new work in us!!!

PRAYER

Lord, we come to You today humbled at the very idea that You would be waiting on us. We are so stained with sin and do not deserve Your gracious love. We realize how important our prayers are and we ask that You increase our desire to talk with You about anything and everything. Please use the time that we have together to strengthen our faith and make us better vessels for Your Work. Amen.

DAY 23 - BE STILL & WAIT

MAIN POINT

He said to them, "It is not for you to know times or seasons that the Father has fixed by his own authority." **Acts 1:7 (ESV)**

WAIT:

We live in a time when our expectations for everything are immediate. When I got my license, if I wanted to go see a movie that night, I had to look in the phone book for the local theater's phone number, call the number, sit and listen to a list of every movie playing and all of their times for the day just to find the one that I was looking for. Nowadays, we can just take out our smart phones, Google the movie we want to see, and where it is playing that is the closest to our location, get the time and BOOM--all done. I can even order the tickets from my phone so that I don't have to stand in line and wait.

Let's say that I am looking for a specific product that I need asap. All that I need to do is Google the product and the store nearest me, and I don't have to drive to five different places to look for it. I can even have them pull the item and have it ready for me when I get there. Not to mention using Amazon to send things to me the very next day so that I don't have to go in the store or even leave my house to get what I need.

I remember the days when I had to call my friend at home and leave a message, and then wait for them to get home, get my message, and call me back just to see if they wanted to come over.

Now, we have text messages that immediately send questions to people whether they are home or not.

What has happened is that we, as a society have grown to expect INSTANT GRATIFICATION! We are so used to being able to do what we want in the here and now that when we are required to wait for something...anything, we feel as though we are getting a raw deal.

There have been many times in life that I have requested clarity or help from God only to find that He wasn't answering in my time frame. I begin to get frustrated when I pray the same prayer over and over with no response. Something that He is teaching me in my own life is that His timing isn't the same as mine. He isn't bound by the constraints of my expectations. He is God and His timing is perfect. So, whether waiting is convenient for me isn't of concern to Him.

He doesn't want me to be in pain or miserable, but He has a plan through the waiting. He is teaching me lessons not only through Scripture and prayer, but through my circumstances and other Christians that He has placed in my life. He is showing me that I need to be faithful and trust Him through the waiting, and often that I am not in a place where I can handle the answer to my prayer yet. I might think that I am, but He knows that I need to grow in my Spiritual maturity more and then He will show me the plan. And let's be real here, sometimes His answer is NO. I know that's hard to hear, but what we think is best sometimes isn't. He can see the entire picture, while we can only see a small portion.

SCRIPTURE

Throughout Scripture, when God told people to wait, it wasn't for a couple of hours or days, it was years! Let's consider this for a bit.

- Abraham - waited 25 years to have a son after God promised Him one (Genesis)

- Moses - waited over 40 years for the Israelites to enter the Promised Land, only to see it from afar because of a previously committed sin. (Exodus)

- Israelites - waited in the wilderness for 40 years (Exodus) Jacob - Waited 7 years to marry Rachel only to be tricked into marrying Leah, and then another 7 years to be able to marry Rachel. (Genesis)

- Joseph - waited 23 years between his dream to the fulfillment of God's promise. (Genesis)

These are just some of the many Biblical examples of God keeping His promises, but man having to wait for the fulfillment. One of the most important things to note about this is that God used the "waiting period" in each of these people's lives to change their hearts toward Him.

LIFE APPLICATION

"Come to me, all you who are weary and burdened, and I will give you rest. Take my yoke upon you and learn from me, for I am gentle and humble in heart, and you will find rest for your souls. For my yoke is easy and my burden is light." ***Matthew 11:28-30 (NIV)***

BE STILL:

Recently I was in a waiting period where it seemed like I could get no answer from God other than "Wait! Just BE STILL!" Being someone who gets things done, I couldn't understand why He would have me wait when I was clearly ready to do whatever it was the He had for me to do. Why wouldn't He just give me directions? I realized after the waiting period was over that God was using that time to prepare me for what was next. I needed to be ready and mature enough in Him before He gave me what was next.

Now it was not easy to sit through that two-year period knowing that His plan is perfect, and I need to be patient. There were many, many times that I felt frustrated and even angry with God. Each time that this happened, I found that my entire life was affected. I had very little joy and peace during these times because I was not in right standing with my Heavenly Father. I was living as though my own way was best and God just didn't understand. But God fully understands the emotions of His people. Every single one of those times that I strayed, He brought me back and reminded me that He doesn't want me to hurt. He wants me to trust Him for the timing, but He also wants me to come to Him with my anxieties and struggles. He doesn't want to be sidelined until His plan comes to fulfillment. He wants to help me now.

"The Lord is close to the brokenhearted and saves those who are crushed in spirit." ***Psalm 34:18 (NIV)***

"He heals the brokenhearted and binds up their wounds." ***Psalm 147:3 (NIV)***

"He will wipe every tear from their eyes. There will be no more death' or mourning or crying or pain, for the old order of things has passed away." ***Revelation 21:4 (NIV)***

We've all had those times when we just don't know what to do or where to turn. We can't see a way out of a situation, and we come to God to ask for His help only to be told to be patient. But He wants us to see that when we are worried, He is there to help, when we are grieving, He is there, and when we are struggling to find the words to say, He already knows them.

Jesus told Martha in Luke 10:38-42, "Martha you are worried about many things, but only one thing is important. Mary has chosen the right thing and it will not be taken from her."

Anybody remember what Mary was doing to "choose the right thing?" Sitting at the feet of Jesus and listening to Him. She was not running around in a panic or worrying herself sick, she was being still. I don't mean literally not moving, but sometimes just turn off the background music in the car and talk to Him. Turn off the TV or the cell phone and spend time with Him. Take the time to go outside and look at the beauty of all that He has created. And you know what?

Over time, by doing these things, I have looked up and realized that my relationship with Jesus is far deeper now than it has ever been before. We need to do this, not only when we are stressed, but regularly rest at the feet of Jesus and let His peace that passes all understanding comfort and refresh our spirit.

If He is the Lord of my life, that makes me His servant. So, anytime that I don't know the answer, I will wait until He tells me. I will try not to go ahead of Him, but to wait on my Lord.

"Wait for the Lord; be strong and take heart and wait for the Lord. ***Psalm 27:14 (NIV)***

PRAYER

Dear Lord, thank You for always caring about the details of our lives. Not only do You love us enough to better us, but You care about every tear that we shed. We love You and thank You for giving us the ability to come directly to You for comfort. Help us to remember amid our busy lives to take time and turn off all distractions and spend time with You just because we want to be near You. In Jesus' Name we pray, Amen.

"Patience is not simply the ability to wait – it's how we behave while we're waiting."

~ Joyce Meyer ~

DAY 24 - CHOOSE WISELY

MAIN POINT

Being around the wrong kind of people can cause their bad qualities to seep into you. The more that you hang around these people, the more that their habits will become yours.

"Do not be misled: "Bad company corrupts good character." **1 Corinthians 15:33 (NIV)**

"Walk with the wise and becomes wise, for a companion of fools suffers harm." **Proverbs 13:20 (NIV)**

You may think that you can change them. But with the state of the world right now it is more likely that you will be pressured into the opposite. So, when you are deciding on whether to make someone your friend, consider this; will they help strengthen your walk with the Lord or hurt it? And will you help theirs or will you be drawn into their activities and behaviors?

The best friends are prayerful friends – they will give godly advice without telling the world. The closest friends that I have, are friends that I call when I am in trouble and I need someone to listen. These are the same women that give Godly advice when I most need it and even when I don't want it. They are your true friends that the Lord placed in your life for a reason. They are the ones that will stop whatever their day has thrown at them and pray with you and for you when you ask and even when you don't. They are the ones that stand at your back when the world is threatening to knock you over and prop you up while the Lord fights your battles. They are the ones that you must pray for as well. They need encouragement and love and Christian counsel trials of their own and God has placed you in their path for that very reason. He has chosen you to help them keep their head up when things around them are shaky. He has chosen you to remind them of the promises that He has made them when they can't see how to make it through one more day.

"Two are better than one, because they have a good return for their labor: If either of them falls down, one can help the other up." ***Ecclesiastes 4:9-12 (NIV)***

SCRIPTURE

"As iron sharpens iron, so one person sharpens another." ***Proverbs 27:17 (NIV)***

Let's look at some biblical examples:

- David & Jonathan – there for each other, protective, loved the Lord
- Elijah & Elisha –sharpened each other, taught each other, loved one another
- Ruth & Naomi – built each other up in difficult times

Now let's look at the opposite side:

- Samson & Delilah – lies & deceit, manipulation
- Job & his friends – they told Job to curse God. They didn't believe that he was innocent of wrongdoing.
- Jesus & Judas – Judas betrayed Jesus for money turning Him into the very people that were going to kill Him.
- Ahithophel & David – Ahithophel was supposed to be a trusty counselor but gave poor advice, spread false rumors about, and eventually betrayed David

The greatest friendships are those that are centered around the love of Jesus. Friends that pray together, stay together! Walking through this life with Godly counsel is a sure-fire way to stay focused on His Will rather than our own.

PRAYER

Heavenly Father, thank You for providing us with the fellowship of friends. We are so thankful that You know our every need before we do. We ask that You help us to befriend the people that You say that should be in our inner circle so that we can make sure that in every aspect of our lives, we are following Your path. Help us to be the encouragement that they need in their lives as well. In Jesus' name we pray, Amen.

DAY 25 - A WILLING HEART

MAIN POINT

In my three years as the Children's Director of my local church, I was responsible, along with a committee, for recruiting volunteers to do various tasks and responsibilities throughout the ministry. This included Sunday School, Children's Church, the AWANA program, and Vacation Bible School. As it is in many churches, 20% of people do 80% of the work and my volunteers were getting burnt out from serving in so many different capacities. That 20% were always willing to step up when needed and teach the children about having a relationship with Jesus. But one year, I remember that they'd begun to get weary. I couldn't blame them; I was exhausted too. We were trying to pour from an empty cup. They needed a break, and to be spiritually fed themselves. That year, my partner and I knew that we would need to think outside the box to fill all the positions for the upcoming Vacation Bible School. In the end, we rallied the troops and got every position filled except for the Preschool Worship Rally and Preschool Crafts. These positions required approximately 20 minutes of each night, so if we could find someone to lead in those areas, those people could then go to their own classes after serving.

We decided to go to the group that I have found to be the most eager and willing people of the church, the Youth Group. I'll admit, I was a little nervous, but considering that each class would have their regular teachers in these activities to help, we decided to give it a go.

I asked two trustworthy young ladies to lead the worship session for the young kids, and then two others to lead the crafts. I assured them that we would provide everything including directions, and that the crafts were very simple, and the teachers would be there to assist. I was blown away by their passion for serving the Lord and the children of our church. They didn't hesitate for one second. They had helped their parents with this age in Children's Church before, and they were confident that they were the right ones for the job. That was by far the easiest recruitment that I have experienced and remains to this day something that I am reminded of when I think about having a willing heart. This was such a positive experience that the youth still help with these classes during Vacation Bible School, even now.

Their first reaction wasn't fear of how they would look, or whether they would know enough, they knew that God would give them the ability and confidence to complete the task. Jesus said that we are to be like little children when we come to Him. I know that middle and high school kids are not "little children" any longer, but they chose to serve the Lord with hearts as innocent and eager as little children. God used them not only to fill a need, but to also set an example for the rising youth in the years to come.

"Don't let anyone look down on you because you are young, but set an example for the believers in speech, in conduct, in love, in faith and in purity." ***1 Timothy 4:12 (NIV)***

SCRIPTURE

"Behold, I stand at the door and knock. If anyone hears my voice and opens the door, I will come into him and eat with him, and he with me." ***Revelation 3:20 (ESV)***

To the church at Corinth, Paul wrote the letters of 1 & 2 Corinthians. This was a church that Paul had led the establishment of felt much affection toward. He spoke very passionately in all his letters, but we very clearly see his connection to Corinth.

In 2 Corinthians 9, Paul encouraged the church on their service to the Lord. He said in verse Chapter 9, Verse 2 that he knows about their eagerness to help and that he has boasted about them in Macedonia. As Paul spoke to the Macedonians, he began to witness a ripple effect. The people of Macedonia developed a desire to have the same joy and gladness in their service as well.

"For I know your readiness, of which I boast about you to the people of Macedonia, saying that Achaia has been ready since last year. And your zeal has stirred up most of them." ***2 Corinthians 9:2 (ESV)***

WHAT DOES IT MEAN TO HAVE A WILLING HEART?

We must put God first in our lives. When we make Him our first priority, then we develop a desire to please Him and with that comes a willingness to do His work.

"And you shall love the Lord your God with all your heart and with all your soul and with all your mind and with all your strength." ***Mark 12:30 (ESV)***

We WANT to serve Him because we LOVE Him, not begrudgingly or because we feel like we HAVE to.

"Serve the Lord with gladness! Come into his presence with singing!" ***Psalm 100:2 (ESV)***

"But thanks be to God that, though you used to be slaves to sin, you have come to obey from your heart the pattern of teaching that has now claimed your allegiance. " ***Romans 6:17 (NIV)***

WHY SHOULD WE HAVE A WILLING HEART?

We need to properly share The Gospel with the lost from a place of gratitude rather than treating it as a chore.

“Do your best to present yourself to God as one approved, a worker who has no need to be ashamed, rightly handling the word of truth." ***2 Timothy 2:15 (ESV)***

God can see our reasons for doing things. We cannot hide anything from Him. He is always searching us and testing our motives.

"The heart is deceitful above all things, and desperately sick; who can understand it? "I the Lord search the heart and test the mind, to give every man according to his ways, according to the fruit of his deeds." ***Jeremiah 17:9-10 (ESV)***

"But the Lord said to Samuel, "Do not look on his appearance or on the height of his stature, because I have rejected him. For the Lord sees not as man sees: man looks on the outward appearance, but the Lord looks on the heart." ***1 Samuel 16:7 (ESV)***

We will receive rewards in Heaven if we serve Him with all our hearts.

"If you are willing and obedient, you shall eat the good of the land." ***Isaiah 1:19 (ESV)***

We want to be able to stand before Him on that glorious day and hear the words of pride from our Heavenly Father.

"His master replied, 'Well done, good and faithful servant! You have been faithful with a few things; I will put you in charge of many things. Come and share your master's happiness!' ***Matthew 25:21 (NIV)***

<u>WHAT CAN WE LEARN FROM THIS?</u>

- We need to be ready and eager to do the work of the Lord.
- We are an example to those around us. Not only in person, but even to those that are hundreds or thousands of miles away.
- God works through us powerfully when we are willing to be used.

- We need to have the desire to do His Will, but we need to actually complete the work as well.

"So now finish doing it as well, so that your readiness in desiring it may be matched by your completing it out of what you have." **2 Corinthians 8:11 (ESV)**

God is preparing us for His future plans. He wants us to be ready not only in desire, but in action as well. We need to be ready and willing when He gives us the go-ahead.

He will give us the will and the ability. If we don't have the desire yet, we can pray for it. If we have the desire but don't yet have the will, then we can pray for it as well. God grants freely to those that ask according to His plan and purpose!

PRAYER

Lord, we come to You today knowing that we are far from perfect. We are constantly messing up and coming back for forgiveness and we thank You that You always wipe the slate clean. Father, as we close out this week, we pray that You would increase our desire to do Your Will above all things. Help us to make You our number one priority and that You will give us the will to complete the tasks that You set before us without fear or hesitancy. We want to serve You Lord. Please guide our steps to remain on the path of righteousness. In Jesus' Name we pray, Amen.

WEEK 6 - BE ON GUARD

MAIN POINT

"Be sober-minded; be watchful. Your adversary the devil prowls around like a roaring lion, seeking someone to devour." ***1 Peter 5:8 (ESV)***

The enemy is always there, tempting and trying to trip us up. He wants to destroy our relationship with Jesus. He wants to keep us as far away from the Lord as possible. Anything that he can do to keep us from spreading The Gospel is what he will do. He knows our weaknesses; he knows our thoughts. He knows exactly what to come at us with that is the most likely to cause me to sin.

This week, we are going to go over a few of the things that we need to be careful about. These are things that can potentially harm our fellowship with our Heavenly Father.

- Be on guard against the world
- Be on guard against our sinful nature.
- Be on guard when dealing with technology.
- Watch what we say.
- Be on guard against how failure makes us feel.

Satan is running rampant in the world that we live in. He is putting lies out there that directly go against the Word of God. He prowls around just waiting for the opportunity to strike. We must not let our guard down. We must be ready to go to battle against the evil all around us. We are different. We are children of God. We have had our eyes opened to the truth, but we are not immune to sin. We are forgiven and made new, but we still must watch our step to stay on the righteous path.

The world is constantly changing. Things what were absolutely spoken out against 20 years ago are being praised in the streets today, and it will be worse in 20 more years. But God never changes. His Word is the same today as it was when He inspired it to be written. We must say rooted in Jesus and His eternal truth so that we won't be tricked and devoured by the enemy.

How do we do that?

- BE PREPARED - be realistic. Know that we are still human and subject to sinfulness. Be aware of our weaknesses and remain ready with a plan for defense when temptation comes.

- PUT ON THE ARMOR OF GOD - when we awake in the morning, let's pray for God to protect our minds and hearts as we seek to serve Him that day.

- PRAY - constantly be in a state of prayer with the Lord.

- STAY IN THE WORD - Memorize verses to help us when we are amid an attack.

- ALWAYS HAVE HIS WORDS ON YOUR HEART AND MIND - immerse ourselves in Him.

- DON'T GIVE IN TO PRESSURE - surround ourselves with other Christians who understand and will support us in our weaknesses and encourage us to stay strong.

PRAYER

Father, please help us to stand strong in our faith in you. Remind us to not be surprised when the enemy attacks, but rather to always be on guard waiting and watching so that we can be ready to battle and stay right with You. In Jesus' Name, Amen.

DAY 26 - THE WORLD

MAIN POINT

When Adam and Eve tasted the apple in the Garden of Eden, sin became a part of the world. Not one of us is immune. Even Jesus Himself faced temptation in the wilderness. The devil tempted Jesus with food, power, fame, and wealth. But He fought temptation with Scripture and prevailed pure and clean. He never sinned, not once. He is and will always be the only man to remain sinless and perfect, thereby making him the perfect sacrifice to pay for our sins.

"For by one sacrifice he has made perfect forever those who are being made holy." ***Hebrews 10:14 (NIV)***

The rest of us are wretched sinners, and because of this it is impossible for us to have fellowship with the Lord. That is why God sent His Son Jesus to die for us. His perfect and pure blood paid the price for all our wrongs. He paid the debt that we deserve so that our sin could be forgiven. Now we can have a relationship with God because Jesus stands in the middle as our advocate claiming us as His own.

Even though we are forgiven of our past, present, and future sins, that sin nature still lives inside of us and Satan is ready to pounce at the first opportunity that we let our guard down. But the Holy Spirit within us has started to change us at our core. He is molding and shaping us into a vessel that the Father can use to tell others about Jesus. He makes us not want to sin anymore, because we now know that sin separates us from our loving Savior. Even now, we still must ask for forgiveness when we do wrong and turn from that sin. This is not because we have lost our Salvation-- that is not possible, once saved, always saved, -- but so that our relationship with God will not become long-distant again. If we allow the sins in our lives to take over our thoughts and priorities without repenting, then God won't remain our priority and our fellowship with Him won't be as intimate as it should be.

For example:

- If we have an argument with a parent and say things we shouldn't or lose our temper and yell at them, the thought of this doesn't go away until we make it right by apologizing. Our parents love us unconditionally, and that doesn't change with our or their mood, but it can affect how close we are with them if we let things fester that we need to make right.
- If things are tense with our spouse, and we don't talk it out and ask each other for forgiveness, then our marital relationship can be affected.

It is the same with God. He loves us unfathomably more than our parents or spouses, but when we sin against God by doing something that isn't right, it can cause a rift in our friendship with him. A rift that if not fixed by forgiveness can lead to our relationship not being as close as it once was.

The fact that we sin will never change. The devil causes sin to run rampant in our world, he wants us to leave God behind. He is roaming freely about Earth trying to use any and every temptation to make us sin. He has caused the world to conform to the idea that "everybody should do what they want when they want." But the reality is that the standards that were set by God of what is right and wrong has not changed. His Word tells us what is good and bad, and we must use that as our baseline of truth. We cannot go against His truth and still expect to reap the benefits of God's blessings and joy.

"Do not conform to the pattern of this world but be transformed by the renewing of your mind. Then you will be able to test and approve what God's will is – his good, pleasing and perfect will." ***Romans 12:2 (NIV)***

WHAT KINDS OF THINGS ARE OF THE WORLD?

MATERIAL THINGS: Thinking of ours or someone else's worth based on what they have or what they look like. The Lord looks at the heart of a person and not their outward appearance.

"Charm is deceptive, and beauty is fleeting; but a woman who fears the Lord is to be praised." ***Proverbs 31:30 (NIV)***

SINS OF THE FLESH: Doing what feels good rather than what is right.

"Do not love the world or the things in the world. If anyone loves the world, the love of the Father is not in him. For all that is in the world—the desires of the flesh and the desires of the eyes and pride in possessions—is not from the Father but is from the world. And the world is passing away along with its desires, but whoever does the will of God abides forever." ***1 John 2:15-17 (ESV)***

BEING UNKIND TO OTHERS:

"This is how we know what love is: Jesus Christ laid down his life for us. And we ought to lay down our lives for our brothers and sisters. If anyone has material possessions and sees a brother or sister in need but has no pity on them, how can the love of God be in that person? Dear children, let us not love with words or speech but with actions and in truth." ***1 John 3:16-18 (NIV)***

SELFISH AMBITION:

"Do not love the world or the things in the world. If anyone loves the world, the love of the Father is not in him. For all that is in the world—the desires of the flesh and the desires of the eyes and pride in possessions—is not from the Father but is from the world. And the world is passing away along with its desires, but whoever does the will of God abides forever. ***1 John 2:15-17 (ESV)***

PERFECTIONISM:

"And he said to them, "You are those who justify yourselves before men, but God knows your hearts. For what is exalted among men is an abomination in the sight of God." ***Luke 16:15 (ESV)***

SCRIPTURE

Satan uses the world to tear us down and make us question God's goodness and love. Here are some of the thoughts that he can send through our heads and how we can combat them with Scripture.

"I AM NOT GOOD ENOUGH"

TRUTH: "But he said to me, "My grace is sufficient for you, for my power is made perfect in weakness." Therefore, I will boast all the more gladly of my weaknesses, so that the power of Christ may rest on me." **2 Corinthians 12:9 (NIV)**

You are more than enough. He made you the way He did for a reason. Anything that you cannot do, He will give you strength for.

"I AM NOT SPECIAL"

TRUTH: "Indeed, the very hairs of your head are all numbered. Don't be afraid; you are worth more than many sparrows. **Luke 12:7 (NIV)**

Your Heavenly Father loves you says that you are unique. You have your own likes and dislikes, strengths and weaknesses. You are one of a kind!

"I AM WEAK"

TRUTH: "He gives strength to the weary and increases the power of the weak." **Isaiah 40:29 (NIV)**

Your weaknesses show His Power. Trust Him to lift you up and give you rest.

"I AM UGLY"

TRUTH: "You are altogether beautiful, my love; there is no flaw in you." **Song of Solomon 4:7 (NIV)**

You were made perfectly by the Lord Almighty. How can you look at the sky and its wonder and beauty and then look at yourself and think anything less? Both were created made by the same Maker.

"I CAN'T DO ANYTHING RIGHT"

TRUTH: "I can do all this through him who gives me strength." **Philippians 4:13 (NIV)**

You are a child of the Almighty God. He can move mountains. Let Him move yours.

"I AM A FAILURE"

TRUTH: "And the God of all grace, who called you to his eternal glory in Christ, after you have suffered a little while, will himself restore you and make you strong, firm and steadfast." **1 Peter 5:10 (NIV)**

We are going to fail. How do we deal with disappointment? By giving up, or by admitting weakness and asking God to use His power to help us?

"I AM ALONE"

TRUTH: "Fear not, for I am with you; be not dismayed, for I am your God; I will strengthen you, I will help you, I will uphold you with my righteous right hand." **Isaiah 41:10 (NKJV)**

He will never leave you or forsake you. When you feel alone, try and take a few minutes to be still and pray for Him to reveal Himself.

Earth was created by God as a place of perfection, but when sin entered the world, everything changed. It seems as if sin is worse than ever, but the truth is that it has always been this bad, now we just hear about it more often because everything is on the internet.

Once we accept Jesus as Lord and Savior, we should no longer feel "at home" here. We should feel as if we are in the world but not of the world. We need to remain this way, because when we become unfazed by the sins of the world, then we are not where we should be with Jesus.

"I have given them your word and the world has hated them, for they are not of the world any more than I am of the world. My prayer is not that you take them out of the world but that you protect them from the evil one. They are not of the world, even as I am not of it." ***John 17:14-16 (NIV)***

Being a follower of Jesus will make us an enemy of the world. It's not easy to admit sinfulness, and they will hate the messengers. We WILL encounter persecution if we proclaim His Name as Lord. Are we willing to be hated by the world, to be in love with Jesus?

PRAYER

Lord, it is a fallen world that we find ourselves living in. We used to be like those lost people that think they belong here, but we are so thankful that You have changed our hearts and saved our souls. Thank you for opening our eyes to help us see the truth. Give us courage as we do Your work here, so that we will not fear in telling everyone about You, so that many more can know the truth of The Gospel. In Jesus' Precious Name I pray. Amen.

DAY 27 - SINFUL NATURE

MAIN POINT

We cannot live as if we are perfect. We must bear in mind that we are still human and therefore sin lives within us, prowling and ready to pounce on us at every opportunity. We need to live knowing the truth of our stains, but confident in the blood of Jesus that continues to pour over us each day to make us clean again. We must be ready to protect ourselves from sin when temptation comes at us and remember that it is not by our own doing that we received forgiveness, it was only by the grace of God.

How can we do this?

"Put to death, therefore, whatever belongs to your earthly nature: sexual immorality, impurity, lust, evil desires, and greed which is idolatry." ***Colossians 3:5 (NIV)***

Turn our backs on the things of the world that we know are wrong and remain focused on the goodness and purity of Jesus.

SCRIPTURE

One of the most prominent names of the Bible is David. He was a man after God's own heart, meaning he had a good heart and wanted to please the Lord. However, he, like the rest of us, was a sinner.

Let's read the beginning of that account in 2 Samuel 11:2-5.

David stayed in Jerusalem while the other kings went off to war. One night he ran into Bathsheba, the wife of Uriah the Hittite, and he began to ask around about her. He found out that she was married, but he gave into the temptation to have sex with her and she became pregnant.

When David heard that Bathsheba was married, it did not stop him from sleeping with her. God made it clear that we should only have physical intimate relations with the husband that He chooses for us. Is this always easy? No, but God wants us to remain pure of heart and flesh so that we can serve Him fully with nothing standing in the way of our fellowship.

There is always a cause and effect. This helps us to remember that we need to be careful about ALL our decisions and not make them when we are not clear headed. What may seem like a little decision, can have an impact on our future. In this case the consequences of their adultery led to a pregnancy for Bathsheba.

David was caused Bathsheba to commit adultery. She did not come to him until he called for her. While she made her own decisions and she will be held responsible before the Lord, we are commanded not to cause one another to sin.

"If anyone causes one of these little ones--those who believe in me--to stumble, it would be better for them to have a large millstone hung around their neck and to be drowned in the depths of the sea." ***Matthew 18:6 (NIV)***

At this point, David could have gone to the Lord, admitted his fault, and been forgiven, like we all have the option to do. Did he choose to do this?

Let's find out. Read 2 Samuel 11: 6-24.

David devised a scheme to get Uriah to come home from war and sleep with his wife so that everyone would think that Bathsheba was pregnant with Uriah's child. Twice David tried to get Uriah to go home to his wife, but it didn't work.

David then decided to send Uriah back to war and put him in the front line where the battle was the most dangerous. He also told his friend Joab to leave Uriah to die when he is injured. David was guilty of murder.

Often, when we sin and don't admit fault and make it right, we have to commit more sins to cover up the first. This is how it was with David. He chose to go on sinning because he was afraid of the consequences of the first sin.

Later in 2 Samuel 12, the prophet Nathan was sent by the Lord to rebuke David because of his sin. God told of the punishments that were to come from David's choices. When Nathan relayed what the Lord had told him, David realized what he'd done had been wrong. God forgave David, but the punishment was that the child born to David and Bathsheba would die. Because the Lord loved David, He later gave them a son together who would one day become the next king of Israel.

Even when we mess up, He still loves us. He has blessed us far beyond what we could ever deserve, but the consequences are still there. They don't go away just because we realize we made a mistake.

This all started because of temptation. When David saw Bathsheba, he became overwhelmed by her beauty. He couldn't think clearly enough to consider this decision. He gave in to what the flesh wanted.

What kinds of things does Satan use to tempt you?

____

We are all tempted by Satan. He is crafty, tricky and knows our weaknesses. The best way to combat him is by repeating scripture to yourself to stay focused when you feel like you could give in. We need to pray and ask your Heavenly Father to reveal to you any temptations that are standing in the way of your fellowship with Him.

There are many to choose from and we all have our weaknesses that make us more apt to sin than others.

LIFE APPLICATION

For a long time, mine was cigarettes. I started when I was 15 when I was trying to be "cool" and it continued for a long time. I used it as a stress reliever when having a bad day. When I met Jesus and He took over my life, I felt a conviction about this sin, and I knew that He was calling me to let go of the crutch. I would quit for a while and then something stressful would happen and I would start back again. This went on and on for many years. I would do well for a while and keep my focus on the Lord, but eventually something would happen, and I would give in to the temptation. My need for nicotine was standing in the way of me being fully dependent on Him. He wanted to be my source of peace in times of stress.

Eventually God opened my eyes to see that smoking was hindering my relationship with him. I was making it like an idol. The first thing I did in the morning should have been thanking the Lord for another day of life, not running outside to smoke. The last thing before bed, should have been my quiet time with Him, not going outside.

This coincided with a time in my life that God was preparing me to become the woman He intended. Yes, I was saved, but I wasn't living as if He was my All in All. He was getting ready to lead me down a road where I could no longer afford to be distracted by the temptations from the world. He had a plan and my sin was standing in the way. Over time, He gave me the strength and power to stop for good. That was 6 years ago. I have since prayed that He will never allow me to put anything above His importance in my life again. We should all ask Him to help us keep a steady head when temptation comes our way, pray for help not to let the world overwhelm us with material things, and remain steadfast in our dedication to keep Him first in our lives. We all need His help to run the race of life with endurance and focus to keep Him as our source of strength.

"No temptation has overtaken you except what is common to mankind. And God is faithful; he will not let you be tempted beyond what you can bear. But when you are tempted, he will also provide a way out so that you can endure it." ***1 Corinthians 10:13 NIV***

Whatever your temptations are today, you can rest in the promises that God offers in that verse. Yes, you will be tempted to sin. You are a sinner by nature, but it's not hitting you any harder than it hits everyone else. God is faithful to give you a way to withstand the temptations that you face. He will not let you be tempted beyond what you can handle.

What can we do to protect ourselves from this temptation?

Read Ephesians 6:10-24.

The Armor of God - In order to resist the devil, it says that we should arm ourselves as if we are going into battle. Essentially, we are going to battle against the dark powers of the world (sin). We need to put on our armor each day to fight against the enemy.

- Belt of Truth – truth so that we don't fall for the world's beliefs
- Breastplate of Righteousness – be honest and humble, good, and kind
- Readiness for the Gospel of Peace – peace with God during trouble
- Shield of Faith – Trust in His promises
- Helmet of Salvation – Be Saved by accepting Jesus as your Savior
- Sword of the Spirit – Be in the Word of God. Read your Bible!

What do we do when we mess up?

There is no way around it, we are going to mess up sometimes no matter how hard we try not to. When we sin, we need to go back to God and confess our sin and ask for forgiveness and help to do right next time.

PRAYER

Lord, thank you for forgiving us of our sins. Help us when we mess up to come to you for help to truly repent. Remind us to put on the armor that You promise will fight off temptation and battle against the evil in this world. In Jesus's name, Amen.

DAY 28 - TECHNOLOGY

MAIN POINT

In today's day and age, technology is very easily accessible. We carry it around on our hips or in our purses everywhere we go. It seems foreign to be without our phones, and we even get frustrated when we don't have WI-FI to hook up to. Kids as young as one-year old walk around with I-pads in their hands and run into walls because they aren't paying attention to where they are going. Video games have come to look so real that it is often difficult to tell if you are watching a live basketball game or someone playing a game. Facebook, Twitter, and Instagram are the most popular ways to get our opinion out into the world, and it only takes the touch of a button. Don't get me wrong, I use technology as much as anyone. There is nothing wrong with technology in and of itself, but when we begin to use to sin, or when we put electronics in a position of more importance than our Savior, we have made them an idol, and that is a problem. The Bible says that Satan will use anything possible to get us off track. Let's see what the Bible says about it.

SCRIPTURE

Technology on its own is cool and convenient, but when combined with our sinful nature, it can become a stumbling block to our Christian walk. We must guard our hearts and minds against the temptations from the enemy and set our focus on Godly things rather than the things of this world.

"Set your mind on things above, not on earthly things." ***Colossians 3:2 (NIV)***

FOR ENTERTAINMENT:

"For the mouth speaks what the heart is full of." ***Matthew 12:34 (NIV)***

The Bible says that what is in the heart eventually comes out of the mouth. So, when we spend our time listening to songs or watching videos about sex, drugs, and with bad language they can become a poison in our minds causing us to become numb to things that are supposed to make us uncomfortable, and eventually they overflow from us. We want the lost to see the Holy Spirit flowing from us, not the sins of the world. We are called to stand apart and we need to be very careful about what we let our thoughts revolve around.

"Above all else, guard your heart, for everything you do flows from it." ***Proverbs 4:23 (NIV)***

FOR SOCIAL MEDIA:

Social media causes conflicts ALL.THE.TIME!!! Whether you are an adult or a teenager, people always want to post their opinions and sometimes that can make other people mad. People even post things on others' pages under a different name so that no one will know who really wrote the comment. Things that we post innocently could be misconstrued and then someone is offended. All I can say is that we have got to be on guard constantly when on social media. I mean, we are putting things out there in writing for potentially the entire world to see, not to mention that colleges, employers, teachers, and coaches check out the social media pages of teenagers before they decide whether you are allowed to be a part of their program.

I am not suggesting that we should be worried about offending people with our faith. That is the one area that we should not feel nervous about stating the truth, but we must do it in a loving way rather than out of judgment. In other words, we shouldn't be quick to put people down because of their sin but show them love as Jesus did. No matter a person's sin, He loves them, and they still need to know that. And remember that He forgives us freely for the things that we do wrong as well. Is our sin so much worse than theirs, that we deserve compassion and they don't?

"What causes fights and quarrels among you? Don't they come from your desires that battle within you? You desire but do not have, so you kill. You covet but cannot get what you want, so you quarrel and fight." ***James 4:1-2 (NIV)***

Satan uses the newest and coolest technology to reach us because he wants to tear apart our relationships with God. He causes us to compare our material wealth with others, which can make us or someone else feel "less than" others. Can you think of a time when you have compared your "stuff" with someone else's? Of course, we all have. The problem comes when we can't find contentment with the stuff that we already have.

SIN WITHOUT INTENTION:

We also need to be careful about what we allow ourselves to see. Let's say that we Google something for research only to be sent to a site filled with pornography. Obviously, this was by accident, but if we continue to hang around the site or come back to it, this is where the problem starts. We must remember who we belong to and that we are no longer part of this world.

"You were taught, with regard to your former way of life, to put off your old self, which is being corrupted by its deceitful desires; to be made new in the attitude of your minds; and to put on the new self, created to be like God in true righteousness and holiness." ***Ephesians 4:22-24 (NIV)***

Believe it or not, the world was moving before these technological advances were invented. Back then, we had to call someone on a phone stuck to the wall or in a closed booth. We even wrote letters! Sin was just as much a part of the world now as it was then, it just comes in different packages. The bottom line is that in everything we say, think, and do we must do it for the Glory of God and if that's not happening then we need to reassess our priorities.

If God is speaking to you today, and you feel that you need to start putting God in His rightful place, it might help to fast from it for a bit. We don't just fast from food. We can fast from anything that takes our attention off the Lord. When we take all distractions away and focus solely on the ways of the Lord, our perspective will be righted again.

Spend some time in prayer today, asking for the Holy Spirit to soften your heart to any adjustments that need to be made and to open your eyes to the wonders of the world that are right in front of you rather than on a screen.

PRAYER

Lord, if there is anything in us that is not devoted to You completely, open our eyes to it today. Show us where to improve and give us the strength to change it. Protect our hearts from the enemy so that we can stay in right standing with You. Thank You Father. Amen.

DAY 29 - THE TONGUE

MAIN POINT

Ever heard or said the phrase "sticks and stones may break my bones, but words will never hurt me?" I repeated it like a mantra many times throughout my childhood. Whenever a kid said something mean and I didn't have any "comebacks," I would rely on that old saying. But the truth is that words can hurt more and the pain last longer than even the worst physical pain. Once words are uttered and the thought is out in the open, the cat is out of the bag and there is no putting it back in. You can't hit the undo button and have a re-do. It is done and no matter how badly we feel, we have said something that we regret.

In the moment we are angry or hurt back and just want to strike out to make them feel as badly as we do. Sometimes we aren't mad, but just don't think before we speak and before we know it, we've said something that we never intended to say. In moments like this, people sometimes joke that we put our foot in our mouths, but the truth is that the words that we say should never be taken lightly. The Bible says that it is impossible to tame.

"All kinds of animals, birds, reptiles, and sea creatures are being tamed and have been tamed by mankind, but no human being can tame the tongue. It is a restless evil, full of deadly poison." ***James 3:7-8 (NIV)***

WHAT IS THE PROBLEM?

I often wonder if I were to record the words that I say to my kids and my husband every day, what would I think when I listened to them? Would I be surprised at how I speak to the people that mean the most to me? Would I be ashamed? Am I showing them the love that God extends to me daily like patience, kindness, and unconditional love? Do I show them how proud I am of them, or do they constantly replay my critical words in their heads?

One person in my life that typically thinks before she speaks is my mom. She is the most encouraging and supportive person in my life, hands down. In her mind, I am the greatest, smartest, funniest daughter in the entire world and there is nothing that I cannot do if I put my mind to it. When I call to tell her good news, her response is "Of course you did!"

These words have followed me through my life and remind me when I feel discouraged that there is someone that thinks I am pretty awesome. She never doubts my abilities and always encourages me to keep going, no matter the obstacle. Of course, there are sometimes that I need to get my butt in gear, and she will tell me that too, but always in way that expresses her affection. I want to be like that to the people around me. A person that they can come to when they need a positive word, but also someone that will tell them the truth in a way that shows my love and support for them.

When we realize the depth of our sin and ask Jesus for forgiveness, He doesn't yell at us for being so bad that we can't get into Heaven on our own. He mercifully and graciously grants forgiveness and salvation. He simply opens His arms and lets us in. He wipes away our sins and we start anew...and He carried my debt on that cross! We are the reason that He was there, we are the ones that caused His pain and suffering, and yet He welcomes us. What an amazing love! How many times do we spew words of hatred toward someone just for pulling out in front of us in traffic?

SCRIPTURE

Let's go over some insights about this from God's Holy Word.

"Let no corrupting talk come out of your mouths, but only such as is good for building up, as fits the occasion, that it may give grace to those who hear." ***Ephesians 4:29 (ESV)***

We are to be encouraging and gracious to others as God is gracious to us.

"I tell you, on the day of judgment people will give account for every careless word they speak." ***Matthew 12:36 (ESV)***

We will answer to the Lord for every word that we say, so let's make every word that we say bring glory to Him!

"A soft answer turns away wrath, but a harsh word stirs up anger." ***Proverbs 15:1 (ESV)***

You catch more flies with honey than vinegar. If we speak humbly to people, we are less likely to cause anger.

"Bless those who persecute you; bless and do not curse them." ***Romans 12:14 (ESV)***

Jesus prayed for the forgiveness of those that were beating and killing Him, shouldn't we follow His lead?

LIFE APPLICATION

Have you tried to put toothpaste back into the tube? It's impossible. The same goes for our words! No matter how much we apologize or how much we vow to never do it again, that thought that you had is now out of your head and into someone else's.

WHAT CAN I DO?

- Don't gossip or make fun of other people. All that it does is make others hurt and us look cruel.

- Adjust your tone and refrain from sarcasm. It's not only the words that we say, but how we say them that can sting.
- Take a breath and count to ten before speaking.
- Think about whether the words that you are getting ready to say will benefit anyone involved or are you just aiming to wound?
- Find a Bible verse about taming the tongue to recite in your head whenever you get the urge to say something in anger.

"But now you must put them all away: anger, wrath, malice, slander, and obscene talk from your mouth..." ***Colossians 3:8 (ESV)***

We need to fill our heads and hearts with Godly thoughts rather than worldly things so that when we open our mouths it won't be hate that we speak, but generosity and love.

Let's take the verse below and pray it from our hearts to God's ears that He may grant us the self-control needed to show kindness and love.

"Let the words of my mouth and the meditation of my heart be acceptable in your sight, O Lord, my rock and my redeemer." ***Psalm 19:14 (ESV)***

PRAYER

Dear Lord, thank You for showing us the importance of our words today. Please search our hearts and mold our thoughts to be acceptable to You. Let the words that we speak show people the way to You. Thank You for all the blessings that You have given us, and we praise You for saving us. In Jesus' Name I pray, Amen.

"Let us not love with words or speech but with actions and in truth."

~ 1 John 3:18 ~

DAY 30 - FAILURE

MAIN POINT

We are not and never will be perfect until we enter Heaven and Jesus makes us whole and perfect. We WILL mess up and sometimes we WILL fail at meeting our expectations. So, how do we deal with our mistakes and failures? Do we give up and think badly of ourselves, or do we allow Jesus to pick us up, forgive us, and restore us so that we can move forward?

"It is for freedom that Christ has set us free. Stand firm, then, and do not let yourselves be burdened again by a yoke of slavery." ***Galatians 5:1 (NIV)***

Let's look at a biblical example of a failure in Peter's life and see what insights we can gain.

SCRIPTURE

Read Matthew 26:33-35.

"Peter replied, "Even if all fall away on account of you, I never will."

"Truly I tell you Jesus answered, "This very night, before the rooster crows, you will disown me three times." But Peter declared, "Even if I have to die with you, I will never disown you." And all the other disciples said the same."

Woah! Nobody ever wants to hear that they will fail, especially when your Savior is the one predicting it. That had to be a huge shock for Peter. I wonder if he was worried about it or if he continued believing that he would not fall short.

In life, we spend a lot of time worrying about failure. Am I going to get a good grade on that test? Am I going to get into college? Am I going to perform well in the game today? Not only do we worry but can live in fear about the possibility of not meeting at our goals. As if our failures say something about who we are at our core. In times like this, we must remember that we are not defined by what the world says about us, but by what Jesus says and He says that we are worthy. Not because of our own "work" but because He loves us…EVEN IN FAILURE.

Matthew 6:27 "Can anyone of you by worrying add a single hour to your life?"

1 John 4:18 "There is no fear in love. But perfect love drives out fear, because fear has to do with punishment. The one who fears is not made perfect in love."

Both above verses speak to the issue of fear and worry. The Bible says that nothing good can come from worrying. It's not like we can add any time to our lives by being anxious.

Then, in 1 John 4, it says that if fear is a worry of punishment, then we have nothing to fear once we are perfected in love by Jesus.

Think about it. He already saved us from the punishment that we deserved. By His grace, he provided a way that we didn't have to suffer for our failures. So why spend time and energy fearing it.

Read Matthew 26:69-75.

"Now Peter was sitting out in the courtyard, and a servant girl came to him. "You also were with Jesus of Galilee," she said. But he denied it before them all. "I don't know what you're talking about, he said." Then he went out to the gateway, where another servant girl

saw him and said to the people there, "This fellow was with Jesus of Nazareth." He denied it again, with an oath: "I don't know the man!" After a little while, those standing there went up to Peter and said, "Surely you are one of them; your accent gives you away." Then he began to call down curses, and he swore to them, "I don't know the man!" Immediately a rooster crowed. Then Peter remembered the word Jesus had spoken: "Before the rooster crows, you will disown me three times." And he went outside and wept bitterly."

This is where it happened, the prediction came true. Peter denied Jesus 3 times. I imagine that when that rooster crowed, and Peter realized the seriousness of the offense that he was completely humbled and ashamed. I can imagine him weeping because He had just turned his back on the One that loved him the most.

But just as we do, Peter received restoration from Jesus for what happened.

Now let's move over and read John 21:15-19.
At this point, Jesus had been crucified and raised to life on the third day. This was the third time that He had appeared to the disciples.

"When they had finished eating, Jesus said to Simon Peter, "Simon son of John, do you love me more than these?" "Yes, Lord," he said, "you know that I love you." Jesus said, "Feed my lambs." Again Jesus said, "Simon son of John, do you love me?" He answered, "Yes, Lord, you know that I love you." Jesus said, "Take care of my sheep."

The third time he said to him, "Simon son of John, do you love me?" Peter was hurt because Jesus asked him the third time, "Do you love me?" He said, "Lord, you know all things; you know that I love you." Jesus said, "Feed my sheep. Very truly I tell you, when you were younger you dressed yourself and went where you wanted; but when you are old you will stretch out your hands, and someone else will dress you and lead you where you do not want to *go." Jesus said this to indicate the kind of death by which Peter would glorify God. Then he said to him, "Follow me!"*

LIFE APPLICATION

It wasn't by coincidence that the Lord asked Peter the same question three times. It was to remind Peter gently of his mistake, but at the same time to restore him. Jesus knew that Peter would be the rock on which the New Testament church was built. God had a HUGE plan prepared for hím and He knew that Peter would need to be brave and courageous, but first he needed to be humbled and corrected with love. So now the Messiah who has correctly predicted Peter's betrayal, is telling Peter that eventually following Jesus would lead to his death. But Jesus needed to prepare Peter for what was to come. How often do we need to know that we are forgiven and redeemed? I do every day and I thank my Savior, that even in our mistakes that He welcomes my return.

Sometimes bad things happen to good people. In this life, things are not perfect. Sin is in the world. Whoever said that "an easy life produces growth?" Nobody. The hard times in life lead to change. Changes that God uses to mold and shape who we are and solidify our resolve. It shows where our loyalties lie by where we turn in difficult times.

'But he said to me, "My grace is sufficient for you, for my power is made perfect in weakness." Therefore, I will boast all the more gladly of my weaknesses, so that the power of Christ may rest on me. That is why, for the Christ's sake, then, I delight in weaknesses, in insults, in hardships, in persecutions, in difficulties. For when I am weak, then I am strong.' ***2 Corinthians 12:9-10 (NIV)***

The more that we CANNOT do something, it shows the world God's POWER because He can do it easily.

PRAYER

Most Gracious Heavenly Father, we thank You for Your might, and for our weaknesses. For through our struggles, You are given the glory when we succeed and when we need to be restored. Help us to come to You when we mess up and ask for forgiveness but let us not forget that we have no reason to fear for You have already saved us from the punishment. Thank you, Lord!

"Don't let failure or disappointment cut you off from God or make you think that the future is hopeless. When God closes one door, He often opens another door – if we seek it."

~ Billy Graham ~

SOURCES

WEEK 1:
Graham, B. (2018). 38 Inspirational Quotes from Billy Graham [Article]. https://www.skipprichard.com/

Merriam Webster's Collegiate Dictionary, 10th ed. (Springfield, MA: Merriam-Webster, 1993)

WEEK 2:
Sala, D. (2015). You Are More Precious Than Diamonds [Article]. https://proverbs31.org

Spurgeon, C.H (2018). The 104 Greatest Most Profound Charles Spurgeon Quotes [Article]. www.theblazingcenter.com

WEEK 3:
Covey, S. (2018). 40 Inspirational Stephen Covey Quotes on Success [Article]. https://www.awakenthegreatnesswithin.com

WEEK 4:
Chan, F, (2012). Multiply: Disciples Making Disciples

Groeschel, C. (2014). The Christian Atheist: When You Believe in God but Live as If He Doesn't Exist

Churchill, W., (2015). 50 Greatest Quotes from Winston Churchill [Article]. https://www.theinspiringjournal.com/

Graham, B., (2018). 40 Courageous Quotes from Evangelist Billy Graham [Article]. https://www.crosswalk.com

WEEK 5:
Eyring, H., (2012). Sharing the Gospel Heart to Heart [Article]. https://www.churchofjesuschrist.org/

Munger, R.B., (1999). My Heart, Christ's Home. Having a Mary Heart in a Martha World.

Meyer, J. (1995). Battlefield of the Mind: Winning the Battle in Your Mind

WEEK 6:
Graham, B., (2018) Powerful Faith Filled Billy Graham Quotes [Article]. https://www.thinkaboutsuchthings.com/